Traeger Grill & Smoker

Cookbook 2022

The Complete Guide to Master Your Traeger Wood Pellet Grill with 200 Tasty Recipes for Beginners and Advanced User

Michael T. Welsh

CONTENT

Introduction... 1

Traeger Grill 101 2

Beef,pork & Lamb Recipes 5

Competition Style Bbq Pork Ribs 6
Lamb Shank 6
Santa Maria Tri-tip 7
Deliciously Spicy Rack Of Lamb................................. 7
Bbq Breakfast Grits 8
Easy-to-prepare Lamb Chops 8
Aromatic Herbed Rack Of Lamb................................. 9
Smoked Rack Of Lamb 9
Southern Sugar-glazed Ham 10
Lamb Breast 10
Traeger Beef Short Rib Lollipop 11
Stunning Prime Rib Roast 11
Roasted Whole Ham In Apricot Sauce 12
Buttermilk Pork Loin Roast.. 12
Cowboy Cut Steak.. 13
Wood Pellet Smoked Brisket 13
Smoked Pork Tenderloin 14
Blackened Steak... 14
Roasted Pork With Blackberry Sauce 15
Smoked New York Steaks 15
Smoked Trip Tip With Java Chophouse 16
Roasted Pork With Balsamic Strawberry Sauce 16
Smoked Midnight Brisket... 17
Bbq Sweet Pepper Meatloaf...................................... 17

Reverse-seared Steaks.. 18
Drunken Beef Jerky 18
Strip Steak With Onion Sauce 19
Bacon-wrapped Sausages In Brown Sugar............... 19
Roast Beef... 20
Simple Grilled Lamb Chops....................................... 20
Smoked Longhorn Cowboy Tri-tip 21
Wood Pellet Grilled Bacon... 21
Wood Pellet Grill Pork Crown Roast.......................... 22
Simply Delicious Tri Tip Roast................................... 22
Smoked Apple Bbq Ribs 23
Barbecued Tenderloin.. 23
Smoked Beef Ribs.. 24
Pork Belly Burnt Ends.. 24
Classic Pulled Pork.. 25
Leg Of A Lamb 25
Supper Beef Roast 26
Texas-style Beef Ribs.. 26
Midweek Dinner Pork Tenderloin............................... 27
Texas Shoulder Clod 27
St. Patrick Day's Corned Beef 28
Wine Braised Lamb Shank... 28
Smoked Porchetta With Italian Salsa Verde.............. 29
Wood Pellet Grill Deli-style Roast Beef 30

Poultry Recipes 31

Game Day Chicken Drumsticks.................................. 32
Smo-fried Chicken 32
Savory-sweet Turkey Legs 33
Applewood-smoked Whole Turkey 33
Smoked Cornish Chicken In Wood Pellets................ 34
Garlic Parmesan Chicken Wings............................... 34
Authentic Holiday Turkey Breast 35
Wood Pellet Smoked Spatchcock Turkey.................. 35
Paprika Chicken 36

Crispy & Juicy Chicken... 36
Smoked Chicken Drumsticks...................................... 37
Serrano Chicken Wings.. 37
Budget Friendly Chicken Legs................................... 38
Wood Pellet Grilled Chicken...................................... 38
Bbq Half Chickens 39
Buffalo Chicken Flatbread 39
Sweet Sriracha Bbq Chicken..................................... 40
Wood Pellet Smoked Spatchcock Turkey.................. 40

Cinco De Mayo Chicken Enchiladas 41

Spatchcocked Turkey 41

Wood Pellet Chile Lime Chicken 42

Buffalo Chicken Wraps 42

Jamaican Jerk Chicken Quarters 43

South-east-asian Chicken Drumsticks..................... 43

Smoked And Fried Chicken Wings......................... 44

Wood Pellet Chicken Breasts 44

Bacon-wrapped Chicken Tenders........................... 45

Wood Pellet Grilled Buffalo Chicken Leg 45

Wood Pellet Grilled Buffalo Chicken....................... 46

Smoked Turkey Wings....................................... 46

Smoked Whole Chicken 47

Herb Roasted Turkey.. 47

Skinny Smoked Chicken Breasts 48

Cajun Chicken 48

Smoked Turkey Breast....................................... 49

Ultimate Tasty Chicken...................................... 49

Thanksgiving Dinner Turkey 50

Chinese Inspired Duck Legs................................ 50

Barbecue Chicken Wings 51

Wood-fired Chicken Breasts 51

Smoking Duck With Mandarin Glaze 52

Sweet And Spicy Smoked Wings 52

Smoked Fried Chicken 53

Wood Pellet Smoked Cornish Hens 53

Maple And Bacon Chicken 54

Fish And Seafood Recipes 55

Blackened Catfish.. 56

Lively Flavored Shrimp...................................... 56

Flavor-bursting Prawn Skewers............................ 57

Lemon Garlic Scallops....................................... 57

Citrus-smoked Trout 58

Smoked Scallops... 58

Wine Infused Salmon 59

Oysters In The Shell... 59

Grilled Tilapia.. 60

Grilled Tuna.. 60

Super-tasty Trout.. 61

Sriracha Salmon... 61

Grilled Lingcod.. 62

Cider Salmon.. 62

Teriyaki Smoked Shrimp.................................... 63

Jerk Shrimp 63

Cod With Lemon Herb Butter 64

Wood Pellet Grilled Salmon Sandwich.................... 64

Omega-3 Rich Salmon 65

Grilled Shrimp Scampi...................................... 65

Wood Pellet Grilled Lobster Tail 66

Togarashi Smoked Salmon.................................. 66

Wood Pellet Garlic Dill Smoked Salmon 67

Wood Pellet Smoked Buffalo Shrimp 67

Wood Pellet Salt And Pepper Spot Prawn Skewers.. 68

Halibut... 68

Wood-fired Halibut.. 69

Hot-smoked Salmon... 69

Lobster Tails... 70

Chilean Sea Bass.. 70

Grilled Salmon... 71

Mango Shrimp... 71

Crazy Delicious Lobster Tails 72

Cajun-blackened Shrimp.................................... 72

Pacific Northwest Salmon................................... 73

Wood Pellet Teriyaki Smoked Shrimp 73

Grilled Rainbow Trout....................................... 74

Citrus Salmon... 74

Barbeque Shrimp.. 75

Wood Pellet Rockfish 75

Buttered Crab Legs 76

Grilled Blackened Salmon 76

Vegetable & Vegetarian 77

Recipes... 77

Whole Roasted Cauliflower With Garlic Parmesan Butter.. 78

Grilled Baby Carrots And Fennel With Romesco....... 78

Grilled Cherry Tomato Skewers............................ 79

Crispy Maple Bacon Brussels Sprouts 79

Smoked Healthy Cabbage................................... 80

Grilled Ratatouille Salad 80

Roasted Vegetable Medley.................................. 81

Smoked Deviled Eggs 81

Wood Pellet Smoked Acorn Squash......................... 82

Grilled Carrots And Asparagus 82

Georgia Sweet Onion Bake...................................... 83

Grilled Corn With Honey & Butter............................. 83

Wood Pellet Bacon Wrapped Jalapeno Poppers 84

Wood Pellet Grilled Zucchini Squash Spears............ 84

Easy Smoked Vegetables... 85

Wood Pellet Grilled Mexican Street Corn 85

Grilled Potato Salad... 86

Smoked Tofu... 86

Garlic And Herb Smoke Potato................................. 87

Roasted Parmesan Cheese Broccoli........................ 87

Roasted Spicy Tomatoes... 88

Blt Pasta Salad... 88

Wood Pellet Grill Spicy Sweet Potatoes................... 89

Wood Pellet Grilled Asparagus And Honey Glazed Carrots . 89

Potato Fries With Chipotle Peppers 90

Sweet Potato Fries 90

Feisty Roasted Cauliflower.. 91

Sweet Jalapeño Cornbread....................................... 91

Wood Pellet Grilled Vegetables 92

Roasted Veggies & Hummus..................................... 92

Roasted Okra 93

Roasted Root Vegetables... 93

Other Favorite Recipes 94

Grilled Venison Kebab.. 95

Grilled Chili Burger 95

Smoked Teriyaki Tuna 96

Grilled Pepper Steak With Mushroom Sauce............ 96

Mutton Barbecued And Black Dip............................. 97

Special Mac And Cheese 97

Smoked Irish Bacon 98

Fall Season Apple Pie 98

Summer Treat Corn 99

Mouthwatering Cauliflower 99

Cinnamon Sugar Donut Holes................................ 100

Beer-braised Pork Shank 100

Baked Breakfast Casserole 101

Grilled Tuna Burger With Ginger Mayonnaise......... 101

Barbecue Hot Dog 102

Smoked Chuck Roast.. 102

Traeger Smoked Sausage....................................... 103

Twice-baked Spaghetti Squash.............................. 103

Bearnaise Sauce With Marinated London Broil....... 104

Traeger Stuffed Burgers 104

Veggie Lover's Burgers 105

Bison Burgers 105

Roasted Steak... 106

Grilled Lime Chicken 106

Baked Apple Crisp.. 107

Seafood On Skewers... 107

Smoked Pork Cutlets With Caraway And Dill 108

Cornish Game Hens.. 108

Smoked Pork Shoulder.. 109

Grilled Chicken With Lemon & Cumin..................... 109

Spiced Nuts 110

Succulent Lamb Chops 110

Smoked Bananas Foster Bread Pudding 111

RECIPE INDEX INDEX 112

Introduction

Grilling meets a range of primitive desires; what is not to appreciate about the T-bone, softly crispy from the outside & tender, juicy, and pink in the middle? It's no joke that grilling is America's favorite pastime because of the unrivaled taste it imparts to beef, seafood, and vegetables. Everybody, everywhere these days, has a favorite grilling method, custom barbecue, or cookbook, but the final outcome is most often the same: moist, smoky, tasty vegetables and meat grilled on an open fire. The act of lighting a barbecue brings us to our past, encourages us to appreciate the outdoors, and reunites us with the inner cavemen. You do not need a device or high-end rig for the perfect backyard Barbecue this summer; all you need is a basic grill, some beef, & a couple of tricks up the sleeve.

Grilling and smoking are two incredibly flavorful techniques of cooking. They are quite simple, provided you know exactly what to do. If not, the entire process becomes cumbersome and tiring. Do you want to become a pitmaster but don't have any foolproof recipes for grilling and smoking vegetables, poultry, meats, or seafood? Or maybe you want to make the most of the pellet grill you have at home. Perhaps you want to impress your loved ones with exceptional pellet smoking and grilling skills. If any or all of these apply to you, you have chosen the right book!

Traeger Grill & Smoker Cookbook 2022 is a very well-planned guide to all of your grilling needs, both inside and outside your home. Included in this book are many grilling recipes for you to use and enjoy, from typical fares like burgers and steaks to more exotic dishes like curry pulled pork or ginger grilled pineapple.

Apart from the recipes themselves, Traeger Grill & Smoker Cookbook 2022 also includes some helpful pointers on how best to grill different meats and vegetables-everything from what heat level is appropriate for which type of food to how long it should be cooked for at that level before being removed. There are also some pointers on how to prepare your meal ahead of time and how to polish it up before serving.

Traeger Grill & Smoker Cookbook 2022 is a very helpful guide for anyone who wants the flexibility to create many different types of grilling dishes. It also makes it easier to get more out of your Traeger grill and ensures that you will never burn food again.

Traeger Grill 101

Control Panel

While the Traeger Grill is designed to be innovative, operating it is no rocket science. In fact, the standard digital controller or control panel of the Traeger grill is extremely easy to understand, even for someone who is a novice in the kitchen.

1. Temperature Panel: The temperature panel indicates the temperature that you want to maintain while cooking your food. Temperature is displayed in Fahrenheit.

2. Temperature Control Knob: The temperature knob allows you to increase or decrease the temperature in increments of 25 degrees. The temperature range is from 180°F to 375°F. The temperature control knob also comes with options such as Smoke, High Temperature, and Shut Down Cycle.

3. Timer: The latest models of Traeger Grills also comes with a timer so that your food cooks at the proper moment. This option is also especially important as you do not need to be in front of your grill to turn it off.

4. Menu: More advanced Traeger Grills come with a menu setting that allows you to control your grill settings. You can also update the firmware version of your grill so that you can optimize its Wi-Fi connectivity.

How to Use the Traeger Grill

1. Get Used to the Grill

It is important to give yourself some time to learn to use the grill. You may want to try and use the grill as soon as you have assembled it. If you do, stick to simple and basic recipes instead of attempting anything difficult, especially if you are new to grilling. Begin by cooking smaller pieces of meat before cooking something as difficult as a brisket. A brisket usually takes more than 15 hours, so it is not a beginner-friendly dish. Cook chicken, salmon fillets or steak, Cornish hens, pork loin, tenderloin or even steaks. You can also choose inexpensive cuts that can be cooked within a few hours. Keep the cooking simple when you begin using the grill.

2. Know the Grill's Hot Spots

Every pellet grill has its own hot spots, and identifying them will make cooking easier. To check for hot spots, after you season the grill, heat it to the highest temperature to ensure the grill works first. When cooking for the first time, it is ideal to preheat the grill to a medium-

high temperature. Follow the manual if you are unsure of the right temperature.

Once the grill is heated to a cooking temperature, slice white bread and place it across the grill. Wait for a while and flip the slices. Look at the results. The points where the slices are the darkest are where the temperature is the hottest. If you are unsure of where the hottest spots are the next time you use the grill, take a picture and keep it with the grill. This will make things easier when cooking different types of meat on the pellet grill.

3. Meat Should Not Be At Room Temperature

Before you cook meat, do not let it thaw or reach room temperature. No matter what meat you choose to cook, place it on the preheated smoker or grill straight out of the freezer. Most recipes will suggest bringing the meat to room temperature, but do not do this. When you first place the meat on a preheated smoker or grill, its temperature will increase by a few degrees right away. Starting frozen will make it easier to cook the meat the way you want without any hassle.

4. Use a Good Thermometer

Check the temperature of the meat you want to cook

using a thermometer. It is best to invest in a good food-grade thermometer. The thermometer that comes with the grill doesn't always provide reliable readings. If you are unsure of the right thermometer to use, buy a laser-type thermometer. This gives you a better reading than the thermometer present in the wood pellet grill.

5. Use the Searing Capabilities

Every pellet grill comes with different cooking functions, such as searing, baking, roasting and more. Use these features to cook delicious food. Since most grills can reach temperatures of at least 450°F, you can use them to sear meats very quickly. Read the manual carefully to learn the low and high temperatures of the grill.

6. Generate More Smoke

If you want to smoke meat or vegetables, always use low temperatures. The manual will indicate a low and slow range of temperatures you should stick to, and the range is usually between 220 and 280°F. Smoking meats at higher temperatures for prolonged periods can result in overcooking.

7. Reverse Sear the Meat

It is a good idea to smoke any meat you cook to enhance its flavor. After you smoke the meat for a few minutes at a low temperature, increase the temperature of the grill and finish cooking it. This method will sear the meat and leave it with a smoky flavor. It is best to use this technique to cook chicken, prime rib, or thick cuts of meat. This method is called the reverse sear method.

Tips and Tricks

1. Pellet Storage

You have to be vigilant in storing your pellets, especially if you live in a humid climate. Damp or wet pellets will not lead to the best grilling experience—you won't be able to get a fire going. What's worse, damp or wet pellets will damage the auger since it won't be able to rotate and will burn out the motor.

I bought some 5-gallon pails, and my husband went on the hunt for sealing lids since storing your pellets in an open container is counterproductive. We found that screw-on covers work best to keep moisture out, and they're convenient—you won't have to break your fingers trying to pry them open.

2. Temperature Readings

After using your grill a few times, you may notice that the temperature starts to fluctuate quite a bit. This is because of grease and soot build-up on the temperature probe used to regulate the temperature. An effortless way to stop this from happening is to clean the probe and cover it with foil. Consequently, cooking temperature readings will be more accurate.

3. Cover Your Grill

You may think a grill cover isn't necessary, but believe me, it's crucial. Your Traeger grill is an appliance and one with electronics inside to boot! If you want to ensure your pellet smoker's durability, protect it from the elements.

If you can, move your grill under a rooftop after having a barbeque and use a grill cover. You don't want your pellet smoker to stop working suddenly due to water damage.

4. Clean Your Grill

A lot of people fail at keeping their grill clean. This step is crucial to guard against overfilling the firepot and protect against flare-ups. Not to mention that your grill will look brand-new for longer if you care for it in this simple way. I recommend cleaning your Traeger grill after cooking something for an extended period, or after you're done using it for the weekend. If you love cooking greasier foods, you'll have to clean your grill more often. Here are the steps you should follow:

1. 1.Use an all-natural degreaser/cleaner to spray the grill grate and the inside of the chimney.

2. Remove and clean the sides of the grill grates.

3. Throw away the old foil and drip tray liners.

4. Remove the drip tray and heat baffle.

5. Use a vacuum inside the grill and firepot to remove any food particles.

6. Clean the inside of the chimney.

7. Again, use an all-natural degreaser/cleaner to spray the inside and outside of the grill. Wait a few minutes before wiping clean.

8. Put all components back in their place, including the heat baffle, drip tray, and foil liners. You're all set for your next barbeque!

Tip: Avoid using wire brushes as they will scratch your Traeger grill. Heavy-duty paper towels or a cleaning cloth will work nicely.

5. Be Adventurous

This is vital to your grilling success—you won't enjoy your Traeger grill for long if you have to make the same recipes over and over. What's more, you own a 6-in-1 appliance, and you can't let that versatility go unused. In the beginning, as you get used to a pellet grill, you may end up cooking simple meals, but once you feel confident in your grilling abilities, try new things! Don't limit yourself to

cook only traditional barbeque foods—what about making a smoky bean stew in your Traeger grill? Don't worry, later on in this cookbook, you'll see recipes that will spark your adventurous side.

These aren't the only elements that will contribute to your grilling success, but they cover some of the rookie mistakes many people, myself included, make. It put a real downer on my grilling plans!

Answering Your Questions

There may be some technical issues with any appliances, primarily since your Traeger Grill and Smoker work with electricity. Here are some of the most frequently asked questions when it comes to general use and troubleshooting.

1. My grill Isn't Lighting; What Am I Doing Wrong?

This can happen due to the hotrod not heating up, the induction fan not working, or the auger isn't feeding the fire pot with pellets. Use a process of elimination to find the source of the problem.

My Traeger Grill and Smoker Doesn't Want to Power on. Why?

It's usually due to some or other electrical issues. It can be a bad power outlet, a bad extension cord, a blown fuse on the controller, or the GFCI tripped.

2. My Auger Isn't Moving

If you used damp pellets, it might have caused your auger to jam. If that's not the case, the shear pin that holds the motor to the auger may be broken. You can also check if the auger motor is in working order and make sure that it is getting power from the controller.

3. The Induction Fan Isn't Running

If you haven't used your pellet smoker in a while, the grease on the fan base may have seized—give it a spin to loosen it. In addition, check if there is power from the controller to the orange wires. Lastly, make sure there isn't an obstruction keeping your fan from turning.

4. My Grill Is Running Hot on Smoke. Why is This?

The outside weather will play a role in the smoke temperature since it will have to compensate for hotter or colder conditions. It might also be a case of you closing the lid too soon after the grill was started. It is best to leave the top open for at least 10 minutes to give the startup fuel time to burn off.

5. How Long Can I Leave My Traeger Grill Unattended?

It would be best if you kept the hopper at least half full at all times. So, if you know you're grilling at a high temperature, you will have to check on the level of pellets in the hopper regularly. You can expect to use 3 lbs. per hours when cooking at higher temperatures.

2

Beef,pork & Lamb Recipes

Competition Style Bbq Pork Ribs

Servings: 6

Cooking Time: 2 Hours

Ingredients:

- 2 racks of St. Louis-style ribs
- 1 cup Traeger Pork and Poultry Rub
- 1/8 cup brown sugar
- 4 tablespoons butter
- 4 tablespoons agave
- 1 bottle Traeger Sweet and Heat BBQ Sauce

Directions:

1. Place the ribs in working surface and remove the thin film of connective tissues covering it. In a smaller bowl, combine the Traeger Pork and Poultry Rub, brown sugar, butter, and agave. Mix until well combined.
2. Massage the rub onto the ribs and allow to rest in the fridge for at least 2 hours.
3. When ready to cook, turn the Traeger on and set the temperature to 225°F. Use desired wood pellets when cooking the ribs. Close the lid and preheat for 15 minutes.
4. Place the ribs on the grill grate and close the lid. Smoke for 1 hours and 30 minutes. Make sure to flip the ribs halfway through the cooking time.
5. Ten minutes before the cooking time ends, brush the ribs with BBQ sauce.
6. Remove from the grill and allow to rest before slicing.

Lamb Shank

Servings: 6

Cooking Time: 4 Hours

Ingredients:

- 8-ounce red wine
- 2-ounce whiskey
- 2 tablespoons minced fresh rosemary
- 1 tablespoon minced garlic
- Black pepper
- 6 (1¼-pound) lamb shanks

Directions:

1. In a bowl, add all ingredients except lamb shank and mix till well combined.
2. In a large resealable bag, add marinade and lamb shank.
3. Seal the bag and shake to coat completely.
4. Refrigerate for about 24 hours.
5. When ready to cook, turn the Traeger on and set the temperature to 225°F.
6. Arrange the leg of lamb in pallet grill and cook for about 4 hours.

Santa Maria Tri-tip

👥 **Servings: 4**

🕐 **Cooking Time: 45 Minutes To 1 Hours**

Ingredients:

- 2 teaspoons sea salt
- 2 teaspoons freshly ground black pepper
- 2 teaspoons onion powder
- 2 teaspoons garlic powder
- 2 teaspoons dried oregano
- 1 teaspoon cayenne pepper
- 1 teaspoon ground sage
- 1 teaspoon finely chopped fresh rosemary
- 1 (1½ – to 2-pound) tri-tip bottom sirloin

Directions:

1. When ready to cook, turn the Traeger on and set the temperature to 425°F and preheat the grill with the lid closed.
2. In a small bowl, combine the salt, pepper, onion powder, garlic powder, oregano, cayenne pepper, sage, and rosemary to create a rub.
3. Season the meat all over with the rub and lay it directly on the grill.
4. Close the lid and smoke for 45 minutes to 1 hours, or until a meat thermometer inserted in the thickest part of the meat reads 120°F for rare, 130°F for medium-rare, or 140°F for medium, keeping in mind that the meat will come up in temperature by about another 5°F during the rest period.
5. Remove the tri-tip from the heat, tent with aluminum foil, and let rest for 15 minutes before slicing against the grain.

Deliciously Spicy Rack Of Lamb

👥 **Servings: 6**

🕐 **Cooking Time: 3 Hours**

Ingredients:

- 2 tbsp. paprika
- ½ tbsp. coriander seeds
- 1 tsp. cumin seeds
- 1 tsp. ground allspice
- 1 tsp. lemon peel powder
- Salt and freshly ground black pepper, to taste
- 2 (1½-lb.) rack of lamb ribs, trimmed

Directions:

1. When ready to cook, turn the Traeger on and set the temperature to 225°F and preheat with closed lid for 15 minutes.
2. In a coffee grinder, add all ingredients except rib racks and grind into a powder.
3. Coat the rib racks with spice mixture generously.
4. Arrange the rib racks onto the grill and cook for about 3 hours.
5. Remove the rib racks from grill and place onto a cutting board for about 10-15 minutes before slicing.
6. With a sharp knife, cut the rib racks into equal-sized individual ribs and serve.

Bbq Breakfast Grits

👪 Servings: 12 To 15

🕐 Cooking Time: 30 To 40 Minutes

Ingredients:

- 2 cups chicken stock
- 1 cup water
- 1 cup quick-cooking grits
- 3 tablespoons unsalted butter
- 2 tablespoons minced garlic
- 1 medium onion, chopped
- 1 jalapeño pepper, stemmed, seeded, and chopped
- 1 teaspoon cayenne pepper
- 2 teaspoons red pepper flakes
- 1 tablespoon hot sauce
- 1 cup shredded Monterey Jack cheese
- 1 cup sour cream
- Salt
- Freshly ground black pepper
- 2 eggs, beaten
- ⅓ cup half-and-half
- 3 cups leftover pulled pork (preferably smoked)

Directions:

1. When ready to cook, turn the Traeger on and set the temperature to 350°F. Preheat, with the lid closed, to 350°F.
2. On your kitchen stove top, in a large saucepan over high heat, bring the chicken stock and water to a boil.
3. Add the grits and reduce the heat to low, then stir in the butter, garlic, onion, jalapeño, cayenne, red pepper flakes, hot sauce, cheese, and sour cream. Season with salt and pepper, then cook for about 5 minutes.
4. Temper the beaten eggs and incorporate into the grits. Remove the saucepan from the heat and stir in the half-and-half and pulled pork.
5. Pour the grits into a greased grill-safe 9-by-13-inch casserole dish or aluminum pan.
6. Transfer to the grill, close the lid, and bake for 30 to 40 minutes, covering with aluminum foil toward the end of cooking if the grits start to get too brown on top.

Easy-to-prepare Lamb Chops

👪 Servings: 6

🕐 Cooking Time: 12 Minutes

Ingredients:

- 6 (6-oz.) lamb chops
- 3 tbsp. olive oil
- Salt and freshly ground black pepper, to taste

Directions:

1. When ready to cook, turn the Traeger on and set the temperature to 450°F and preheat with closed lid for 15 minutes.
2. Coat the lamb chops with oil and then, season with salt and black pepper evenly.
3. Arrange the chops onto the grill and cook for about 4-6 minutes per side.
4. Remove the chops from grill and serve hot.

Aromatic Herbed Rack Of Lamb

Servings: 3

Cooking Time: 2 Hours

Ingredients:

- 2 tbsp. fresh sage
- 2 tbsp. fresh rosemary
- 2 tbsp. fresh thyme
- 2 garlic cloves, peeled
- 1 tbsp. honey
- Salt and freshly ground black pepper, to taste
- ¼ C. olive oil
- 1 (1½-lb.) rack of lamb, trimmed

Directions:

1. In a food processor, add all ingredients except for oil and rack of lamb rack and pulse until well combined.
2. While motor is running, slowly add oil and pulse until a smooth paste is formed.
3. Coat the rib rack with paste generously and refrigerate for about 2 hours.
4. When ready to cook, turn the Traeger on and set the temperature to 225°F and preheat with closed lid for 15 minutes.
5. Arrange the rack of lamb onto the grill and cook for about 2 hours.
6. Remove the rack of lamb from grill and place onto a cutting board for about 10-15 minutes before slicing.
7. With a sharp knife, cut the rack into individual ribs and serve.

Smoked Rack Of Lamb

Servings: 4

Cooking Time: 1 Hours And 15 Minutes

Ingredients:

- 1rack of lamb rib, membrane removed
- For the Marinade:
- 1lemon, juiced
- 2teaspoons minced garlic
- 1teaspoon salt
- 1teaspoon ground black pepper
- 1teaspoon dried thyme
- ¼ cup balsamic vinegar
- 1teaspoon dried basil
- For the Glaze:
- 2tablespoons soy sauce
- ¼ cup Dijon mustard
- 2tablespoons Worcestershire sauce
- ¼ cup red wine

Directions:

1. Prepare the marinade and for this, take a small bowl, place all the ingredients in it and whisk until combined.
2. Place the rack of lamb into a large plastic bag, pour in marinade, seal it, turn it upside down to coat lamb with the marinade and let it marinate for a minimum of 8 hours in the refrigerator.
3. When ready to cook, turn the Traeger on and fill the grill hopper with flavored wood pellets, power the grill on by using the control panel, select 'smoke' on the temperature dial, or set the temperature to 300°F and let it preheat for a minimum of 5 minutes.
4. Meanwhile, prepare the glaze and for this, take a small bowl, place all of its ingredients in it and whisk until combined.
5. When the grill has preheated, open the lid, place lamb rack on the grill grate, shut the grill and smoke for 15 minutes.
6. Brush with glaze, flip the lamb and then continue smoking for 1 hours and 15 minutes until the internal temperature reaches 145°F, basting with the glaze every 30 minutes.
7. When done, transfer lamb rack to a cutting board, let it rest for 15 minutes, cut it into slices, and then serve.

Southern Sugar-glazed Ham

👥 **Servings: 12 To 15**

🕐 **Cooking Time: 5 Hours**

Ingredients:

- 1 (12- to 15-pound) whole bone-in ham, fully cooked
- ¼ cup yellow mustard
- 1 cup pineapple juice
- ½ cup packed light brown sugar
- 1 teaspoon ground cinnamon
- ½ teaspoon ground cloves

Directions:

1. When ready to cook, turn the Traeger on and set the temperature to 275°F and preheat with the lid closed.
2. Trim off the excess fat and skin from the ham, leaving a ¼-inch layer of fat. Put the ham in an aluminum foil–lined roasting pan.
3. On your kitchen stove top, in a medium saucepan over low heat, combine the mustard, pineapple juice, brown sugar, cinnamon, and cloves and simmer for 15 minutes, or until thick and reduced by about half.
4. Baste the ham with half of the pineapple–brown sugar syrup, reserving the rest for basting later in the cook.
5. Place the roasting pan on the grill, close the lid, and smoke for 4 hours.
6. Baste the ham with the remaining pineapple–brown sugar syrup and continue smoking with the lid closed for another hours, or until a meat thermometer inserted in the thickest part of the ham reads 140°F.
7. Remove the ham from the grill, tent with foil, and let rest for 20 minutes before carving.

Lamb Breast

👥 **Servings: 2**

🕐 **Cooking Time: 2 Hours And 40 Minutes**

Ingredients:

- 1 (2-pound) trimmed bone-in lamb breast
- ½ cup white vinegar
- ¼ cup yellow mustard
- ½ cup BBQ rub

Directions:

1. When ready to cook, turn the Traeger on and set the temperature to 225°F.
2. Rinse the lamb breast with vinegar evenly.
3. Coat lamb breast with mustard and the, season with BBQ rub evenly.
4. Arrange lamb breast in pallet grill and cook for about 2-2½ hours.
5. Remove the lamb breast from the pallet grill and transfer onto a cutting board for about 10 minutes before slicing.
6. With a sharp knife, cut the lamb breast in desired sized slices and serve.

Traeger Beef Short Rib Lollipop

👥 **Servings: 4**

🕐 **Cooking Time: 3 Hours**

Ingredients:

- 4 beef short rib lollipops
- BBQ Rub
- BBQ Sauce

Directions:

1. When ready to cook, turn the Traeger on and set the temperature to 275°F.
2. Season the short ribs with BBQ rub and place them on the grill.
3. Cook for 4 hours while turning occasionally until the meat is tender.
4. Apply the sauce on the meat in the last 30 minutes of cooking.
5. Serve and enjoy.

Stunning Prime Rib Roast

👥 **Servings: 10**

🕐 **Cooking Time: 3 Hours 50 Minutes**

Ingredients:

- 1 (5-lb.) prime rib roast
- Salt, to taste
- 5 tbsp. olive oil
- 4 tsp. dried rosemary, crushed
- 2 tsp. garlic powder
- 1 tsp. onion powder
- 1 tsp. paprika
- ½ tsp. cayenne pepper
- Freshly ground black pepper, to taste

Directions:

1. Season the roast with salt generously.
2. With a plastic wrap, cover the roast and refrigerate for about 24 hours.
3. In a bowl, mix together remaining ingredients and set aside for about 1 hours.
4. Rub the roast with oil mixture from both sides evenly.
5. Arrange the roast in a large baking sheet and refrigerate for about 6-12 hours.
6. When ready to cook, turn the Traeger on and set the temperature to 225°F and preheat with closed lid for 15 minutes. , using pecan wood chips.
7. Place the roast onto the grill and cook for about 3-3½ hours.
8. Meanwhile, preheat the oven to 500°F.
9. Remove the roast from grill and place onto a large baking sheet.
10. Place the baking sheet in oven and roast for about 15-20 minutes.
11. Remove the roast from oven and place onto a cutting board for about 10-15 minutes before serving.
12. With a sharp knife, cut the roast into desired-sized slices and serve.

Roasted Whole Ham In Apricot Sauce

👥 **Servings: 12**

🕐 **Cooking Time: 2 Hours**

Ingredients:

- 8-pound whole ham, bone-in
- 16 ounces apricot BBQ sauce
- 2 tablespoon Dijon mustard
- 1/4 cup horseradish

Directions:

1. When ready to cook, turn the Traeger on and set the temperature to 325°F and let it preheat for a minimum of 15 minutes.
2. Meanwhile, take a large roasting pan, line it with foil, and place ham on it.
3. When the grill has preheated, open the lid, place roasting pan containing ham on the grill grate, shut the grill and smoke for 1 hours and 30 minutes.
4. Meanwhile, prepare the glaze and for this, take a medium saucepan, place it over medium heat, add BBQ sauce, mustard, and horseradish, stir until mixed and cook for 5 minutes, set aside until required.
5. After 1 hours and 30 minutes smoking, brush ha generously with the prepared glaze and continue smoking for 30 minutes until internal temperature reaches 135°F.
6. When done, remove roasting pan from the grill, let rest for 20 minutes and then cut into slices. Serve ham with remaining glaze.

Buttermilk Pork Loin Roast

👥 **Servings: 4-6**

🕐 **Cooking Time: 3-3.5 Hours**

Ingredients:

- 1 (3-3½lb) pork loin roast
- 1-quart buttermilk brine

Directions:

1. Cut out all fat and silver skin of pork roast.
2. Place the roast and buttermilk brine in a 1-gallon sealable plastic bag or brine container.
3. Refrigerate overnight, rotating roast every few hours if possible.
4. Use of Traegers and grills
5. Remove the salted pork roast from the salt water and dry it lightly with a paper towel.
6. In the part where the roast is thickest, incorporate the meat probe
7. When ready to cook, turn the Traeger on and set the temperature to 225°F using apple or cherry pellets.
8. Suck roast for 3 to 3 1/2 hours until internal temperature reaches 145 ° F.
9. Place the roast under a loose foil tent for 15 minutes and carve it towards the grain.

Cowboy Cut Steak

👪 **Servings: 4**

🕐 **Cooking Time: 1 Hours And 15 Minutes**

Ingredients:

- 2 cowboy cut steak, each about 2 ½ pounds
- Salt as needed
- Beef rub as needed
- For the Gremolata:
- 2 tablespoons chopped mint
- 1 bunch of parsley, leaves separated
- 1 lemon, juiced
- 1 tablespoon lemon zest
- ½ teaspoon minced garlic
- ¼ teaspoon salt
- 1/8 teaspoon ground black pepper
- 1/4 cup olive oil

Directions:

1. When ready to cook, turn the Traeger on and set the temperature to 225°F and let it preheat for a minimum of 5 minutes.
2. Meanwhile, prepare the steaks, and for this, season them with salt and BBQ rub until well coated.
3. When the grill has preheated, open the lid, place steaks on the grill grate, shut the grill and smoke for 45 minutes to 1 hours until thoroughly cooked, and internal temperature reaches 115°F.
4. Meanwhile, prepare gremolata and for this, take a medium bowl, place all of its ingredients in it and then stir well until combined, set aside until combined.
5. When done, transfer steaks to a dish, let rest for 15 minutes, and meanwhile, change the smoking temperature of the grill to 450°F and let it preheat for a minimum of 10 minutes.
6. Then return steaks to the grill grate and cook for 7 minutes per side until the internal temperature reaches 130°F.

Wood Pellet Smoked Brisket

👪 **Servings: 10**

🕐 **Cooking Time: 9 Hours**

Ingredients:

- 2 tbsp garlic powder
- 2 tbsp onion powder
- 2 tbsp paprika
- 2 tbsp chili powder
- 1/3 cup salt
- 1/3 cup black pepper
- 12 lb whole packer brisket, trimmed
- 1-1/2 cup beef broth

Directions:

1. When ready to cook, turn the Traeger on and set the temperature to 225°F. Let preheat for 15 minutes with the lid closed.
2. Meanwhile, mix garlic, onion, paprika, chili, salt, and pepper in a mixing bowl.
3. Season the brisket generously on all sides.
4. Place the meat on the grill with the fat side down and let it cool until the internal temperature reaches 160°F.
5. Remove the meat from the grill and double wrap it with foil. Return it to the grill and cook until the internal temperature reaches 204°F.
6. Remove from grill, unwrap the brisket and let est for 15 minutes.
7. Slice and serve.

Smoked Pork Tenderloin

Servings: 4-6

Cooking Time: 1 Hours And 30 Minutes

Ingredients:

- 2 (1½2 pounds) pork fillet
- ¼ Extra virgin olive oil with cup roasted garlic flavor
- ¼Cup Jan's Original Dry Rub or Pork Dry Rub

Directions:

1. When ready to cook, turn the Traeger on and set the temperature to 230°F using hickory or apple pellets.
2. Remove the wrap from the meat and insert a Traeger grill probe or remote meat probe into the thickest part of each tenderloin. If your grill does not have a meat probe or you do not have a remote meat probe, use an instant reading digital thermometer to read the internal temperature while cooking.
3. Place the tenderloin directly on the grill and smoke at 230 ° F for 45 minutes.
4. Raise the temperature of the pit to 350 ° F and finish cooking the tenderloin for about 45 minutes until the internal temperature of the thickest part reaches 145 ° F.
5. Rest the pork tenderloin under a loose foil tent for 10 minutes before serving.

Blackened Steak

Servings: 4

Cooking Time: 60 Minutes

Ingredients:

- 2 steaks, each about 40 ounces
- 4 tablespoons blackened rub
- 4 tablespoons butter, unsalted

Directions:

1. When ready to cook, turn the Traeger on and set the temperature to 225°F and let it preheat for a minimum of 15 minutes.
2. Meanwhile, prepare the steaks and for this, sprinkle rub on all sides of each steak and let marinate for 10 minutes.
3. When the grill has preheated, open the lid, place steaks on the grill grate, shut the grill and smoke for 40 minutes until internal temperature reaches 119°F.
4. When done, remove steaks from the grill and wrap each in a piece of foil.
5. Change the smoking temperature to 400°F, place a griddle pan on the grill grate, and when hot, add 2 tablespoons butter and when it begins to melts, add steak and sear it for 4 minutes per side until internal temperature reaches 125°F.
6. Transfer steaks to a dish and then repeat with the remaining steak.
7. Let seared steaks rest for 10 minutes, then slice each steak across the grain and serve.

Roasted Pork With Blackberry Sauce

Servings: 4

Cooking Time: 50 Minutes

Ingredients:

- 2 lb. pork tenderloin
- 2 tablespoons dried rosemary
- Salt and pepper to taste
- 2 tablespoons olive oil
- 12 blackberries, sliced
- 1 cup balsamic vinegar
- 4 tablespoons sugar

Directions:

1. When ready to cook, turn the Traeger on and set the temperature to 350°F. Preheat the Traeger for 15 minutes while the lid is closed.
2. Season the pork with the rosemary, salt and pepper.
3. In a pan over high heat, pour in the oil and sear pork for 2 minutes per side.
4. Transfer to the grill and cook for 20 minutes.
5. Take the pan off the grill.
6. Let rest for 10 minutes.
7. In a pan over medium heat, simmer the blackberries in vinegar and sugar for 30 minutes.
8. Pour sauce over the pork and serve.

Smoked New York Steaks

Servings: 4

Cooking Time: 1 To 2 Hours

Ingredients:

- 4 (1-inch-thick) New York steaks
- 2 tablespoons olive oil
- Salt
- Freshly ground black pepper

Directions:

1. When ready to cook, turn the Traeger on and set the temperature to 180°F. Preheat the grill, with the lid closed, to 180°F.
2. Rub the steaks all over with olive oil and season both sides with salt and pepper.
3. Place the steaks directly on the grill grate and smoke for 1 hours.
4. Increase the grill's temperature to 375°F and continue to cook until the steaks' internal temperature reaches 145°F for medium-rare.
5. Remove the steaks and let them rest 5 minutes, before slicing and serving.

Smoked Trip Tip With Java Chophouse

👥 **Servings: 4**

🕐 **Cooking Time: 90 Minutes**

Ingredients:

- 2 tbsp olive oil
- 2 tbsp java chophouse seasoning
- 3 lb trip tip roast, fat cap and silver skin removed

Directions:

1. When ready to cook, turn the Traeger on and set the temperature to 225°F.
2. Rub the roast with olive oil and seasoning then place it on the smoker rack.
3. Smoke until the internal temperature is 140°F.
4. Remove the tri-tip from the smoker and let rest for 10 minutes before serving. Enjoy.

Roasted Pork With Balsamic Strawberry Sauce

👥 **Servings: 3**

🕐 **Cooking Time: 35 Minutes**

Ingredients:

- 2 lb pork tenderloin
- Salt and pepper to taste
- 2 tbsp rosemary, dried
- 2 tbsp olive oil
- 12 strawberries, fresh
- 1 cup balsamic vinegar
- 4 tbsp sugar

Directions:

1. When ready to cook, turn the Traeger on and set the temperature to 350°F and preheat for 15 minutes with a closed lid.
2. Meanwhile, rinse the pork and pat it dry. Season with salt, pepper, and rosemary.
3. In an oven skillet, heat oil until smoking. Add the pork and sear on all sides until golden brown.
4. Set the skillet in the grill and cook for 20 minutes or until the meat is no longer pink and the internal temperature is 150°F.
5. Remove the pork from the grill and let rest for 10 minutes.
6. Add berries to the skillet and sear over the stovetop for a minute. Remove the strawberries from the skillet.
7. Add vinegar in the same skillet and scrape any browned bits from the skillet bottom. Bring it to boil then reduce heat to low. Stir in sugar and cook until it has reduced by half.
8. Slice the meat and place the strawberries on top then drizzle vinegar sauce. Enjoy.

Smoked Midnight Brisket

Servings: 6

Cooking Time: 12 Hours

Ingredients:

- 1 tbsp Worcestershire sauce
- 1 tbsp Traeger beef Rub
- 1 tbsp Traeger Chicken rub
- 1 tbsp Traeger Blackened Saskatchewan rub
- 5 lb flat cut brisket
- 1 cup beef broth

Directions:

1. Rub the sauce and rubs in a mixing bowl then rub the mixture on the meat.
2. When ready to cook, turn the Traeger on and set the temperature to 180°F. Preheat your grill to 180°F with the lid closed for 15 minutes. You can use super smoke if you desire.
3. Place the meat on the grill and grill for 6 hours or until the internal temperature reaches 160°F.
4. Remove the meat from the grill and double wrap it with foil.
5. Add beef broth and return to grill with the temperature increased to 225°F. Cook for 4 hours or until the internal temperature reaches 204°F.
6. Remove from grill and let rest for 30 minutes. Serve and enjoy with your favorite BBQ sauce.

Bbq Sweet Pepper Meatloaf

Servings: 8

Cooking Time: 3 Hours And 15 Minutes

Ingredients:

- 1 cup chopped red sweet peppers
- 5 pounds ground beef
- 1 cup chopped green onion
- 1 tablespoon salt
- 1 tablespoon ground black pepper
- 1 cup panko bread crumbs
- 2 tablespoon BBQ rub and more as needed
- 1 cup ketchup
- 2 eggs

Directions:

1. When ready to cook, turn the Traeger on and set the temperature to 225°F and let it preheat for a minimum of 5 minutes.
2. Meanwhile, take a large bowl, place all the ingredients in it except for ketchup and then stir until well combined.
3. Shape the mixture into meatloaf and then sprinkle with some BBQ rub.
4. When the grill has preheated, open the lid, place meatloaf on the grill grate, shut the grill, and smoke for 2 hours and 15 minutes.
5. Then change the smoking temperature to 375°F, insert a food thermometer into the meatloaf and cook for 45 minutes or more until the internal temperature of meatloaf reaches 155°F.
6. Brush the top of meatloaf with ketchup and then continue cooking for 15 minutes until glazed. When done, transfer food to a dish, let it rest for 10 minutes, then cut it into slices and serve.

Reverse-seared Steaks

👥 **Servings: 4**

🕐 **Cooking Time: 1 Or 2 Hours**

Ingredients:

- 4 (4-ounce) sirloin steaks
- 2 tablespoons olive oil
- Salt
- Freshly ground black pepper
- 4 tablespoons butter

Directions:

1. When ready to cook, turn the Traeger on and set the temperature to 180°F. Preheat the grill, with the lid closed.
2. Rub the steaks all over with olive oil and season both sides with salt and pepper.
3. Place the steaks directly on the grill grate and smoke until their internal temperature reaches 135°F. Remove the steaks from the grill.
4. Place a cast-iron skillet on the grill grate and increase the grill's temperature to 450°F.
5. Place the steaks in the skillet and top each with 1 tablespoon of butter. Cook the steaks until their internal temperature reaches 145°F, flipping once after 2 or 3 minutes. (I recommend reverse-searing over an open flame rather than in the cast-iron skillet, if your grill has that option.) Remove the steaks and serve immediately.

Drunken Beef Jerky

👥 **Servings: 6**

🕐 **Cooking Time: 5 Hours**

Ingredients:

- 1 (12-oz.) bottle dark beer
- 1 C. soy sauce
- ¼ C. Worcestershire sauce
- 2 tbsp. hot sauce
- 3 tbsp. brown sugar
- 2 tbsp. coarse ground black pepper, divided
- 1 tbsp. curing salt
- ½ tsp. garlic salt
- 2 lb. flank steak, trimmed and cut into ¼-inch thick slices

Directions:

1. In a bowl, add the beer, soy sauce, Worcestershire sauce, brown sugar, 2 tbsp. of black pepper, curing salt and garlic salt and mix well.
2. In a large resealable plastic bag, place the steak slices and marinade mixture.
3. Seal the bag, squeezing out the air and then shake to coat well.
4. Refrigerate to marinate overnight.
5. When ready to cook, turn the Traeger on and set the temperature to 180°F and preheat with closed lid for 15 minutes.
6. Remove the steak slices from the bag and discard the marinade.
7. With paper towels, pat dry the steak slices.
8. Sprinkle the steak slices with remaining black pepper generously.
9. Arrange the steak slices onto the grill in a single layer and cook for about 4-5 hours.

Strip Steak With Onion Sauce

👥 **Servings: 4**

🕐 **Cooking Time: 1 Hours**

Ingredients:

- 2 New York strip steaks
- Prime rib rub
- ½ lb. bacon, chopped
- 1 onion, sliced
- 1/4 cup brown sugar
- 1/2 tablespoon balsamic vinegar
- 3 tablespoons brewed coffee
- 1/4 cup apple juice

Directions:

1. Sprinkle both sides of steaks with prime rib rub.
2. When ready to cook, turn the Traeger on and set the temperature to 350°F.
3. Preheat for 15 minutes while the lid is closed.
4. Place a pan over the grill.
5. Cook the bacon until crispy.
6. Transfer to a plate.
7. Cook the onion in the bacon drippings for 10 minutes.
8. Stir in brown sugar and cook for 20 minutes.
9. Add the rest of the ingredients and cook for 20 minutes.
10. Grill the steaks for 5 minutes per side.
11. Serve with the onion and bacon mixture.

Bacon-wrapped Sausages In Brown Sugar

👥 **Servings: 8**

🕐 **Cooking Time: 30 Minutes**

Ingredients:

- 1 pound bacon strips, halved
- 14 ounces cocktail sausages
- ½ cup brown sugar

Directions:

1. Place bacon strips on clean working space, roll them by using a rolling pin, and then wrap a sausage with a bacon strip, securing with a toothpick.
2. Place wrapped sausage in a casserole dish, repeat with the other sausages, place them into the casserole dish in a single layer, cover with sugar and then let them sit for 30 minutes in the refrigerator.
3. When ready to cook, turn the Traeger on and set the temperature to 350°F and let it preheat for a minimum of 15 minutes.
4. Meanwhile, remove the casserole dish from the refrigerator and then arrange sausage on a cookie sheet lined with parchment paper.
5. When the grill has preheated, open the lid, place cookie sheet on the grill grate, shut the grill and smoke for 30 minutes.
6. When done, transfer sausages to a dish and then serve.

Roast Beef

👥 **Servings: 8**

🕐 **Cooking Time: 5 Hours**

Ingredients:

- 5 lb. sirloin roast
- 1 tablespoon olive oil
- Prime rib dry rub

Directions:

1. Tie the sirloin roast with kitchen string.
2. Brush the roast with oil and season with dry rub.
3. When ready to cook, turn the Traeger on and set the temperature to 180°F.
4. Roast the beef for 5 hours.
5. Remove the kitchen string.
6. Let cool before slicing thinly.

Simple Grilled Lamb Chops

👥 **Servings: 6**

🕐 **Cooking Time: 6 Minutes**

Ingredients:

- 1/4 cup distilled white vinegar
- 2 tbsp salt
- 1/2 tbsp black pepper
- 1 tbsp garlic, minced
- 1 onion, thinly sliced
- 2 tbsp olive oil
- 2lb lamb chops

Directions:

1. In a resealable bag, mix vinegar, salt, black pepper, garlic, sliced onion, and oil until all salt has dissolved.
2. Add the lamb chops and toss until well coated. Place in the fridge to marinate for 2 hours.
3. When ready to cook, turn the Traeger on and set the temperature to high heat.
4. Remove the lamb from the fridge and discard the marinade. Wrap any exposed bones with foil.
5. Grill the lamb for 3 minutes per side. You can also broil in a broiler for more crispness.
6. Serve and enjoy

Smoked Longhorn Cowboy Tri-tip

Servings: 7

Cooking Time: 4 Hours

Ingredients:

- 3 lb tri-tip roast
- 1/8 cup coffee, ground
- 1/4 cup Traeger beef rub

Directions:

1. When ready to cook, turn the Traeger on and set the temperature to 180°F. Preheat the grill with the lid closed for 15 minutes.
2. Meanwhile, rub the roast with coffee and beef rub. Place the roast on the grill grate and smoke for 3 hours.
3. Remove the roast from the grill and double wrap it with foil. Increase the temperature to 275°F.
4. Return the meat to the grill and let cook for 90 minutes or until the internal temperature reaches 135°F.
5. Remove from the grill, unwrap it and let rest for 10 minutes before serving.
6. Enjoy.

Wood Pellet Grilled Bacon

Servings: 6

Cooking Time: 25 Minutes

Ingredients:

- 1 lb bacon, thickly cut

Directions:

1. When ready to cook, turn the Traeger on and set the temperature to 375°F.
2. Line a baking sheet with parchment paper then place the bacon on it in a single layer.
3. Close the lid and bake for 20 minutes. Flip over, close the lid, and bake for an additional 5 minutes.
4. Serve with the favorite side and enjoy.

Wood Pellet Grill Pork Crown Roast

👥 **Servings: 5**

🕐 **Cooking Time: 1 Hours**

Ingredients:

- 13 ribs pork
- 1/4 cup favorite rub
- 1cup apple juice
- 1 cup Apricot BBQ sauce

Directions:

1. When ready to cook, turn the Traeger on and set the temperature to 375°F and preheat for 15 minutes with the lid closed.
2. Meanwhile, season the pork with the rub then let sit for 30 minutes.
3. Wrap the tips of each crown roast with foil to prevent the borns from turning black.
4. Place the meat on the grill grate and cook for 90 minutes. Spray apple juice every 30 minutes.
5. When the meat has reached an internal temperature of 125°F remove the foils.
6. Spray the roast with apple juice again and let cook until the internal temperature has reached 135°F.
7. In the last 10 minutes of cooking, baste the roast with BBQ sauce.
8. Remove from the grill and wrap with foil. Let rest for 15 minutes before serving. Enjoy.

Simply Delicious Tri Tip Roast

👥 **Servings: 8**

🕐 **Cooking Time: 35 Minutes**

Ingredients:

- 1 tbsp. granulated onion
- 1 tbsp. granulated garlic
- Salt and freshly ground black pepper, to taste
- 1 (3-lb.) tri tip roast, trimmed

Directions:

1. In a bowl, add all ingredients except for roast and mix well.
2. Coat the roast with spice mixture generously.
3. Set aside at room temperature until grill heats.
4. When ready to cook, turn the Traeger on and set the temperature to 250°F and preheat with closed lid for 15 minutes.
5. Place the roast onto the grill and cook for about 25 minutes.
6. Now, set the grill to 350-400°F and preheat with closed lid for 15 minutes. and sear roast for about 3-5 minutes per side.
7. Remove the roast from grill and place onto a cutting board for about 15-20 minutes before slicing.
8. With a sharp knife, cut the roast into slices across the grain and serve.

Smoked Apple Bbq Ribs

👥 **Servings: 6**

🕐 **Cooking Time: 2 Hours**

Ingredients:

- 2 racks St. Louis-style ribs
- ¼ cup Traeger Big Game Rub
- 1 cup apple juice
- A bottle of Traeger BBQ Sauce

Directions:

1. Place the ribs on a working surface and remove the film of connective tissues covering it.
2. In another bowl, mix the Game Rub and apple juice until well-combined.
3. Massage the rub on to the ribs and allow to rest in the fridge for at least 2 hours.
4. When ready to cook, turn the Traeger on and set the temperature to 225°F. Use apple wood pellets when cooking the ribs. Close the lid and preheat for 15 minutes.
5. Place the ribs on the grill grate and close the lid. Smoke for 1 hours and 30 minutes. Make sure to flip the ribs halfway through the cooking time.
6. Ten minutes before the cooking time ends, brush the ribs with BBQ sauce.
7. Remove from the grill and allow to rest before slicing.

Barbecued Tenderloin

👥 **Servings: 4 To 6**

🕐 **Cooking Time: 30 Minutes**

Ingredients:

- 2 (1-pound) pork tenderloins
- 1 batch Sweet and Spicy Cinnamon Rub

Directions:

1. When ready to cook, turn the Traeger on and set the temperature to 350°F. Preheat with the lid closed.
2. Generously season the tenderloins with the rub. Using your hands, work the rub into the meat.
3. Place the tenderloins directly on the grill grate and smoke until their internal temperature reaches 145°F.
4. Remove the tenderloins from the grill and let them rest for 5 to 10 minutes, before thinly slicing and serving.

Smoked Beef Ribs

👪 **Servings: 4 To 8**

🕐 **Cooking Time: 4 To 6 Hours**

Ingredients:

- 2 (2- or 3-pound) racks beef ribs
- 2 tablespoons yellow mustard
- 1 batch Sweet and Spicy Cinnamon Rub

Directions:

1. When ready to cook, turn the Traeger on and set the temperature to 225°F. Preheat the grill with the lid closed.
2. Remove the membrane from the backside of the ribs. This can be done by cutting just through the membrane in an X pattern and working a paper towel between the membrane and the ribs to pull it off.
3. Coat the ribs all over with mustard and season them with the rub. Using your hands, work the rub into the meat.
4. Place the ribs directly on the grill grate and smoke until their internal temperature reaches between 190°F and 200°F.
5. Remove the racks from the grill and cut them into individual ribs. Serve immediately.

Pork Belly Burnt Ends

👪 **Servings: 8 To 10**

🕐 **Cooking Time: 6 Hours**

Ingredients:

- 1 (3-pound) skinless pork belly (if not already skinned, use a sharp boning knife to remove the skin from the belly), cut into 1½- to 2-inch cubes
- 1 batch Sweet Brown Sugar Rub
- ½ cup honey
- 1 cup The Ultimate BBQ Sauce
- 2 tablespoons light brown sugar

Directions:

1. When ready to cook, turn the Traeger on and set the temperature to 250°F. Preheat the grill, with the lid closed.
2. Generously season the pork belly cubes with the rub. Using your hands, work the rub into the meat.
3. Place the pork cubes directly on the grill grate and smoke until their internal temperature reaches 195°F.
4. Transfer the cubes from the grill to an aluminum pan. Add the honey, barbecue sauce, and brown sugar. Stir to combine and coat the pork.
5. Place the pan in the grill and smoke the pork for 1 hours, uncovered. Remove the pork from the grill and serve immediately.

Classic Pulled Pork

👥 **Servings: 8 To 12**

🕐 **Cooking Time: 16 To 20 Hours**

Ingredients:

- 1 (6- to 8-pound) bone-in pork shoulder
- 2 tablespoons yellow mustard
- 1 batch Pork Rub

Directions:

1. When ready to cook, turn the Traeger on and set the temperature to 225°F. Preheat the grill, with the lid closed, to 225°F.
2. Coat the pork shoulder all over with mustard and season it with the rub. Using your hands, work the rub into the meat.
3. Place the shoulder on the grill grate and smoke until its internal temperature reaches 195°F.
4. Pull the shoulder from the grill and wrap it completely in aluminum foil or butcher paper. Place it in a cooler, cover the cooler, and let it rest for 1 or 2 hours.
5. Remove the pork shoulder from the cooler and unwrap it. Remove the shoulder bone and pull the pork apart using just your fingers. Serve immediately as desired. Leftovers are encouraged.

Leg Of A Lamb

👥 **Servings: 10**

🕐 **Cooking Time: 2 Hours And 30 Minutes**

Ingredients:

- 1 (8-ounce) package softened cream cheese
- ¼ cup cooked and crumbled bacon
- 1 seeded and chopped jalapeño pepper
- 1 tablespoon crushed dried rosemary
- 2 teaspoons garlic powder
- 1 teaspoon onion powder
- 1 teaspoon paprika
- 1 teaspoon cayenne pepper
- Salt, to taste
- 1 (4-5-pound) butterflied leg of lamb
- 2-3 tablespoons olive oil

Directions:

1. For filling in a bowl, add all ingredients and mix till well combined.
2. For spice mixture in another small bowl, mix together all ingredients.
3. Place the leg of lamb onto a smooth surface. Sprinkle the inside of leg with some spice mixture.
4. Place filling mixture over the inside surface evenly. Roll the leg of lamb tightly and with a butcher's twine, tie the roll to secure the filling
5. Coat the outer side of roll with olive oil evenly and then sprinkle with spice mixture.
6. When ready to cook, turn the Traeger on and set the temperature to 230°F.
7. Arrange the leg of lamb in pallet grill and cook for about 2-2½ hours. Remove the leg of lamb from pallet grill and transfer onto a cutting board.
8. With a piece of foil, cover leg loosely and transfer onto a cutting board for about 20-25 minutes before slicing.
9. With a sharp knife, cut the leg of lamb in desired sized slices and serve.

Supper Beef Roast

👪 **Servings: 7**

🕐 **Cooking Time: 3 Hours**

Ingredients:

- 3-1/2 beef top round
- 3 tbsp vegetable oil
- Prime rib rub
- 2 cups beef broth
- 1 russet potato, peeled and sliced
- 2 carrots, peeled and sliced
- 2 celery stalks, chopped
- 1 onion, sliced
- 2 thyme sprigs

Directions:

1. Rub the roast with vegetable oil and place it on the roasting fat side up. Season with prime rib rub then pour the beef broth.
2. When ready to cook, turn the Traeger on and set the temperature to 500°F and preheat for 15 minutes with the lid closed.
3. Cook for 30 minutes or until the roast is well seared.
4. Reduce temperature to 225°F. Add the veggies and thyme and cover with foil. Cook for 3 more hours o until the internal temperature reaches 135°F.
5. Remove from the grill and let rest for 10 minutes. Slice against the grain and serve with vegetables and the pan dippings.
6. Enjoy.

Texas-style Beef Ribs

👪 **Servings: 4**

🕐 **Cooking Time: 6 Hours 3 Minutes**

Ingredients:

- 2 tbsp. butter
- 1 C. white vinegar
- 1 C. yellow mustard
- 2 tbsp. brown sugar
- 2 tbsp. Tabasco sauce
- 1 tsp. Worcestershire sauce
- 2 racks of beef ribs
- Salt and freshly ground black pepper, to taste

Directions:

1. For BBQ sauce: in a pan, melt butter over medium heat. Stir in vinegar, mustard, brown sugar, Tabasco and Worcestershire sauce and remove from heat.
2. Set aside to cool completely.
3. When ready to cook, turn the Traeger on and set the temperature to 225°F and preheat with closed lid for 15 minutes.
4. Season the rib racks with salt and black pepper evenly.
5. Coat rib rack with cooled sauce evenly.
6. Arrange the rib racks onto the grill and cook for about 5-6 hours, coating with sauce after every 2 hours.
7. Remove the rib racks from grill and place onto a cutting board for about 10-15 minutes before slicing.
8. With a sharp knife, cut the rib racks into equal-sized individual ribs and serve.

Midweek Dinner Pork Tenderloin

Servings: 6

Cooking Time: 3 Hours

Ingredients:

- ½ C. apple cider
- 3 tbsp. honey
- 2 (1¼-1½-lb.) pork tenderloins, silver skin removed
- 3 tbsp. sweet rub

Directions:

1. In a small bowl, mix together apple cider and honey.
2. Coat the outside of tenderloins with honey mixture and season with the rub generously.
3. With a plastic wrap, cover each tenderloin and refrigerate for about 2-3 hours.
4. When ready to cook, turn the Traeger on and set the temperature to 225°F and preheat with closed lid for 15 minutes.
5. Arrange the tenderloins onto the grill and cook for about 2½-3 hours.
6. Remove the pork tenderloins from grill and place onto a cutting board for about 10 minutes before slicing.
7. With a sharp knife, cut each pork tenderloin into desired-sized slices and serve.

Texas Shoulder Clod

Servings: 16 To 20

Cooking Time: 12 To 16 Hours

Ingredients:

- ½ cup sea salt
- ½ cup freshly ground black pepper
- 1 tablespoon red pepper flakes
- 1 tablespoon minced garlic
- 1 tablespoon cayenne pepper
- 1 tablespoon smoked paprika
- 1 (13- to 15-pound) beef shoulder clod

Directions:

1. In a small bowl, combine the salt, pepper, red pepper flakes, minced garlic, cayenne pepper, and smoked paprika to create a rub. Generously apply it to the beef shoulder.
2. When ready to cook, turn the Traeger on and set the temperature to 250°F. Preheat with the lid closed.
3. Put the meat on the grill grate, close the lid, and smoke for 12 to 16 hours, or until a meat thermometer inserted deeply into the beef reads 195°F. You may need to cover the clod with aluminum foil toward the end of smoking to prevent overbrowning.
4. Let the meat rest for about 15 minutes before slicing against the grain and serving.

St. Patrick Day's Corned Beef

Servings: 14

Cooking Time: 7 Hours

Ingredients:

- 6 lb. corned beef brisket, drained, rinsed and pat dried
- Freshly ground black pepper, to taste
- 8 oz. light beer

Directions:

1. When ready to cook, turn the Traeger on and set the temperature to 275°F and preheat with closed lid for 15 minutes.
2. Sprinkle the beef brisket with spice packet evenly.
3. Now, sprinkle the brisket with black pepper lightly.
4. Place the brisket onto the grill and cook for about 3-4 hours.
5. Remove from grill and transfer briskets into an aluminum pan.
6. Add enough beer just to cover the bottom of pan.
7. With a piece of foil, cover the pan, leaving one corner open to let out steam.
8. Cook for about 2-3 hours.
9. Remove the brisket from grill and place onto a cutting board for about 10-15 minutes before slicing.
10. With a sharp knife, cut the brisket in desired sized slices and serve.
11. Remove the brisket from grill and place onto a cutting board for about 25-30 minutes before slicing.
12. With a sharp knife, cut the brisket in desired sized slices and serve.

Wine Braised Lamb Shank

Servings: 2

Cooking Time: 10 Hours

Ingredients:

- 2 (1¼-lb.) lamb shanks
- 1-2 C. water
- ¼ C. brown sugar
- 1/3 C. rice wine
- 1/3 C. soy sauce
- 1 tbsp. dark sesame oil
- 4 (1½x½-inch) orange zest strips
- 2 (3-inch long) cinnamon sticks
- 1½ tsp. Chinese five-spice powder

Directions:

1. When ready to cook, turn the Traeger on and set the temperature to 225°F and preheat with closed lid for 15 minutes, using charcoal and soaked apple wood chips.
2. With a sharp knife, pierce each lamb shank at many places.
3. In a bowl, add remaining all ingredients and mix until sugar is dissolved.
4. In a large foil pan, place the lamb shanks and top with sugar mixture evenly.
5. Place the foil pan onto the grill and cook for about 8-10 hours, flipping after every 30 minutes. (If required, add enough water to keep the liquid ½-inch over).
6. Remove from the grill and serve hot.

Smoked Porchetta With Italian Salsa Verde

👥 **Servings: 8 To 12**

🕐 **Cooking Time: 3 Hours**

Ingredients:

- 3 Tablespoon dried fennel seed
- 2 Tablespoon red pepper flakes
- 2 Tablespoon sage, minced
- 1 Tablespoon rosemary, minced
- 3 Clove garlic, minced
- As Needed lemon zest
- As Needed orange zest
- To Taste salt and pepper
- 6 Pound Pork Belly, skin on
- As Needed salt and pepper
- 1 Whole shallot, thinly sliced
- 6 Tablespoon parsley, minced
- 2 Tablespoon freshly minced chives
- 1 Tablespoon Oregano, fresh
- 3 Tablespoon white wine vinegar
- 1/2 Teaspoon kosher salt
- 3/4 Cup olive oil
- 1/2 Teaspoon Dijon mustard
- As Needed fresh lemon juice

Directions:

1. Prepare herb mixture: In a medium bowl, mix together fennel seeds, red pepper flakes, sage, rosemary, garlic, citrus zest, salt and pepper.
2. Place pork belly skin side up on a clean work surface and score in a crosshatch pattern. Flip the pork belly over and season flesh side with salt, pepper and half of the herb mixture.
3. Place trimmed pork loin in the center of the belly and rub with remaining herb mixture. Season with salt and pepper.
4. Roll the pork belly around the loin to form a cylindrical shape and tie tightly with kitchen twine at 1" intervals.
5. Season the outside with salt and pepper and transfer to refrigerator, uncovered and let air dry overnight.
6. When ready to cook, turn the Traeger on and set the temperature to Smoke.
7. Fit a rimmed baking sheet with a rack and place the pork on the rack seam side down.
8. Place the pan directly on the grill grate and smoke for 1 hours.
9. Increase the grill temperature to 325°F and roast until the internal temperature of the meat reaches 135°F, about 2 1/2 hours. If the exterior begins to burn before the desired internal temperature is reached, tent with foil.
10. Remove from grill and let stand 30 minutes before slicing.
11. 1To make the Italian salsa verde: Combine shallot, parsley, chives, vinegar, oregano and salt in a medium bowl. Whisk in olive oil then stir in mustard and lemon juice.

Wood Pellet Grill Deli-style Roast Beef

👥 **Servings: 2**

🕐 **Cooking Time: 4 Hours**

Ingredients:

- 4lb round-bottomed roast
- 1 tbsp coconut oil
- 1/4 tbsp garlic powder
- 1/4 tbsp onion powder
- 1/4 tbsp thyme
- 1/4 tbsp oregano
- 1/2 tbsp paprika
- 1/2 tbsp salt
- 1/2 tbsp black pepper

Directions:

1. Combine all the dry hubs to get a dry rub.
2. Roll the roast in oil then coat with the rub.
3. When ready to cook, turn the Traeger on and set the temperature to 185°F.
4. Smoke for 4 hours or until the internal temperature reaches 140°F.
5. Remove the roast from the grill and let rest for 10 minutes.
6. Slice thinly and serve.

3
Poultry Recipes

Game Day Chicken Drumsticks

Servings: 8

Cooking Time: 1 Hours

Ingredients:

- For Brine:
- ½ C. brown sugar
- ½ C. kosher salt
- 5 C. water
- 2 (12-oz.) bottles beer
- 8 chicken drumsticks
- For Coating:
- ¼ C. olive oil
- ½ C. BBQ rub
- 1 tbsp. fresh parsley, minced
- 1 tbsp. fresh chives, minced
- ¾ C. BBQ sauce
- ¼ C. beer

Directions:

1. For brine: in a bucket, dissolve brown sugar and kosher salt in water and beer.
2. Place the chicken drumsticks in brine and refrigerate, covered for about 3 hours.
3. When ready to cook, turn the Traeger on and set the temperature to 275°F and preheat with closed lid for 15 minutes.
4. Remove chicken drumsticks from brine and rinse under cold running water.
5. With paper towels, pat dry chicken drumsticks.
6. Coat drumsticks with olive oil and rub with BBQ rub evenly.
7. Sprinkle the drumsticks with parsley and chives.
8. Arrange the chicken drumsticks onto the grill and cook for about 45 minutes.
9. Meanwhile, in a bowl, mix together BBQ sauce and beer.
10. Remove from grill and coat the drumsticks with BBQ sauce evenly.
11. Cook for about 15 minutes more.
12. Serve immediately.

Smo-fried Chicken

Servings: 4 To 6

Cooking Time: 55 Minutes

Ingredients:

- 1 egg, beaten
- ½ cup milk
- 1 cup all-purpose flour
- 2 tablespoons salt
- 1 tablespoon freshly ground black pepper
- 2 teaspoons freshly ground white pepper
- 2 teaspoons cayenne pepper
- 2 teaspoons garlic powder
- 2 teaspoons onion powder
- 1 teaspoon smoked paprika
- 8 tablespoons (1 stick) unsalted butter, melted
- 1 whole chicken, cut up into pieces

Directions:

1. When ready to cook, turn the Traeger on and set the temperature to 375°F. Preheat with the lid closed.
2. In a medium bowl, combine the beaten egg with the milk and set aside.
3. In a separate medium bowl, stir together the flour, salt, black pepper, white pepper, cayenne, garlic powder, onion powder, and smoked paprika.
4. Line the bottom and sides of a high-sided metal baking pan with aluminum foil to ease cleanup.
5. Pour the melted butter into the prepared pan.
6. Dip the chicken pieces one at a time in the egg mixture, and then coat well with the seasoned flour. Transfer to the baking pan.
7. Smoke the chicken in the pan of butter ("smo-fry") on the grill, with the lid closed, for 25 minutes, then reduce the heat to 325°F and turn the chicken pieces over.
8. Continue smoking with the lid closed for about 30 minutes, or until a meat thermometer inserted in the thickest part of each chicken piece reads 165°F.
9. Serve immediately.

Savory-sweet Turkey Legs

Servings: 4

Cooking Time: 4 To 5 Hours

Ingredients:

- 1 gallon hot water
- 1 cup curing salt (such as Morton Tender Quick)
- ¼ cup packed light brown sugar
- 1 teaspoon freshly ground black pepper
- 1 teaspoon ground cloves
- 1 bay leaf
- 2 teaspoons liquid smoke
- 4 turkey legs
- Mandarin Glaze, for serving

Directions:

1. In a large container with a lid, stir together the water, curing salt, brown sugar, pepper, cloves, bay leaf, and liquid smoke until the salt and sugar are dissolved; let come to room temperature.
2. Submerge the turkey legs in the seasoned brine, cover, and refrigerate overnight.
3. When ready to smoke, remove the turkey legs from the brine and rinse them; discard the brine.
4. When ready to cook, turn the Traeger on and set the temperature to 225°F. Preheat with the lid closed.
5. Arrange the turkey legs on the grill, close the lid, and smoke for 4 to 5 hours, or until dark brown and a meat thermometer inserted in the thickest part of the meat reads 165°F.
6. Serve with Mandarin Glaze on the side or drizzled over the turkey legs.

Applewood-smoked Whole Turkey

Servings: 6 To 8

Cooking Time: 5 To 6 Hours

Ingredients:

- 1 (10- to 12-pound) turkey, giblets removed
- Extra-virgin olive oil, for rubbing
- ¼ cup poultry seasoning
- 8 tablespoons (1 stick) unsalted butter, melted
- ½ cup apple juice
- 2 teaspoons dried sage
- 2 teaspoons dried thyme

Directions:

1. When ready to cook, turn the Traeger on and set the temperature to 250°F. Preheat with the lid closed.
2. Rub the turkey with oil and season with the poultry seasoning inside and out, getting under the skin.
3. In a bowl, combine the melted butter, apple juice, sage, and thyme to use for basting.
4. Put the turkey in a roasting pan, place on the grill, close the lid, and grill for 5 to 6 Hours, basting every hours, until the skin is brown and crispy, or until a meat thermometer inserted in the thickest part of the thigh reads 165°F.
5. Let the bird rest for 15 to 20 minutes before carving.

Smoked Cornish Chicken In Wood Pellets

👪 **Servings: 6**

🕐 **Cooking Time: 1 Hours 10 Minutes**

Ingredients:

- Cornish hens - 6
- Canola or avocado oil - 2-3 tbsp
- Spice mix - 6 tbsp

Directions:

1. When ready to cook, turn the Traeger on and set the temperature to 275°F.
2. Rub the whole hen with oil and the spice mix. Use both of these ingredients liberally.
3. Place the breast area of the hen on the grill and smoke for 30 minutes.
4. Flip the hen, so the breast side is facing up. Increase the temperature to 400°F.
5. Cook until the temperature goes down to 165°F.
6. Pull it out and leave it for 10 minutes.
7. Serve warm with a side dish of your choice.

Garlic Parmesan Chicken Wings

👪 **Servings: 6**

🕐 **Cooking Time: 20 Minutes**

Ingredients:

- 5 pounds of chicken wings
- 1/2 cup chicken rub
- 3 tablespoons chopped parsley
- 1 cup shredded parmesan cheese
- For the Sauce:
- 5 teaspoons minced garlic
- 2 tablespoons chicken rub
- 1 cup butter, unsalted

Directions:

1. When ready to cook, turn the Traeger on and set the temperature to 450°F and let it preheat for a minimum of 15 minutes.
2. Meanwhile, take a large bowl, place chicken wings in it, sprinkle with chicken rub and toss until well coated.
3. When the grill has preheated, open the lid, place chicken wings on the grill grate, shut the grill, and smoke for 10 minutes per side until the internal temperature reaches 165°F.
4. Meanwhile, prepare the sauce and for this, take a medium saucepan, place it over medium heat, add all the ingredients for the sauce in it and cook for 10 minutes until smooth, set aside until required.
5. When done, transfer chicken wings to a dish, top with prepared sauce, toss until mixed, garnish with cheese and parsley and then serve.

Authentic Holiday Turkey Breast

👪 **Servings: 6**

🕐 **Cooking Time: 4 Hours**

Ingredients:

- ½ C. honey
- ¼ C. dry sherry
- 1 tbsp. butter
- 2 tbsp. fresh lemon juice
- Salt, to taste
- 1 (3-3½-pound) skinless, boneless turkey breast

Directions:

1. In a small pan, place honey, sherry and butter over low heat and cook until the mixture becomes smooth, stirring continuously.
2. Remove from heat and stir in lemon juice and salt. Set aside to cool.
3. Transfer the honey mixture and turkey breast in a sealable bag.
4. Seal the bag and shake to coat well.
5. Refrigerate for about 6-10 hours.
6. When ready to cook, turn the Traeger on and set the temperature to 225°F and preheat with closed lid for 15 minutes.
7. Place the turkey breast onto the grill and cook for about 2½-4 hours or until desired doneness.
8. Remove turkey breast from grill and place onto a cutting board for about 15-20 minutes before slicing.
9. With a sharp knife, cut the turkey breast into desired-sized slices and serve.

Wood Pellet Smoked Spatchcock Turkey

👪 **Servings: 6**

🕐 **Cooking Time: 1 Hours And 45 Minutes**

Ingredients:

- 1 whole turkey
- 1/2 cup oil
- 1/4 cup chicken rub
- 1 tbsp onion powder
- 1 tbsp garlic powder
- 1 tbsp rubbed sage

Directions:

1. When ready to cook, turn the Traeger on and set the temperature to High.
2. Meanwhile, place the turkey on a platter with the breast side down then cut on either side of the backbone to remove the spine.
3. Flip the turkey and season on both sides then place it on the preheated grill or on a pan if you want to catch the drippings. Grill on high for 30 minutes, reduce the temperature to 325°F, and grill for 45 more minutes or until the internal temperature reaches 165°F Remove from the grill and let rest for 20 minutes before slicing and serving. Enjoy.

Paprika Chicken

👨‍👩‍👧 Servings: 7

🕐 Cooking Time: 2 – 4 Hours

Ingredients:

- 4-6 chicken breast
- 4 tablespoons olive oil
- 2tablespoons smoked paprika
- ½ tablespoon salt
- ¼ teaspoon pepper
- 2teaspoons garlic powder
- 2teaspoons garlic salt
- 2teaspoons pepper
- 1teaspoon cayenne pepper
- 1teaspoon rosemary

Directions:

1. When ready to cook, turn the Traeger on and set the temperature to 220°F.
2. Prepare your chicken breast according to your desired shapes and transfer to a greased baking dish.
3. Take a medium bowl and add spices, stir well.
4. Press the spice mix over chicken and transfer the chicken to smoker.
5. Smoke for 1-1 and a ½ hours.
6. Turn-over and cook for 30 minutes more.
7. Once the internal temperature reaches 165°F.
8. Remove from the smoker and cover with foil.
9. Allow it to rest for 15 minutes.
10. Enjoy!

Crispy & Juicy Chicken

👨‍👩‍👧 Servings: 6

🕐 Cooking Time: 5 Hours

Ingredients:

- ¾ C. dark brown sugar
- ½ C. ground espresso beans
- 1 tbsp. ground cumin
- 1 tbsp. ground cinnamon
- 1 tbsp. garlic powder
- 1 tbsp. cayenne pepper
- Salt and freshly ground black pepper, to taste
- 1 (4-lb.) whole chicken, neck and giblets removed

Directions:

1. When ready to cook, turn the Traeger on and set the temperature to 200°F and preheat with closed lid for 15 minutes.
2. In a bowl, mix together brown sugar, ground espresso, spices, salt and black pepper.
3. Rub the chicken with spice mixture generously.
4. Place the chicken onto the grill and cook for about 3-5 hours.
5. Remove chicken from grill and place onto a cutting board for about 10 minutes before carving.
6. With a sharp knife, cut the chicken into desired-sized pieces and serve.

Smoked Chicken Drumsticks

Servings: 5

Cooking Time: 2 Hours 30 Minutes

Ingredients:

- 10 chicken drumsticks
- 2tsp garlic powder
- 1tsp salt
- 1tsp onion powder
- 1/2 tsp ground black pepper
- ½ tsp cayenne pepper
- 1tsp brown sugar
- 1/3 cup hot sauce
- 1tsp paprika
- ½ tsp thyme

Directions:

1. In a large mixing bowl, combine the garlic powder, sugar, hot sauce, paprika, thyme, cayenne, salt, and ground pepper. Add the drumsticks and toss to combine.
2. Cover the bowl and refrigerate for 1 hours.
3. Remove the drumsticks from the marinade and let them sit for about 1 hours until they are at room temperature.
4. Arrange the drumsticks into a rack.
5. When ready to cook, turn the Traeger on and set the temperature to 250°F.
6. Close the lid and preheat grill to 250°F, using hickory or apple hardwood pellets.
7. Place the rack on the grill and smoke drumsticks for 2 hours, 30 minutes, or until the drumsticks' internal temperature reaches 180°F.
8. Remove drumsticks from heat and let them rest for a few minutes.
9. Serve.

Serrano Chicken Wings

Servings: 4

Cooking Time: 40 Minutes

Ingredients:

- 4 lb. chicken wings
- 2 cups beer
- 2 teaspoons crushed red pepper
- Cajun seasoning powder
- 1 lb. Serrano chili peppers
- 1 teaspoon fresh basil
- 1 teaspoon dried oregano
- 4 cloves garlic
- 1 cup vinegar
- Salt and pepper to taste

Directions:

1. Soak the chicken wings in beer.
2. Sprinkle with crushed red pepper.
3. Cover and refrigerate for 12 hours.
4. Remove chicken from brine.
5. Season with Cajun seasoning.
6. When ready to cook, turn the Traeger on and set the temperature to 325°F. Preheat your Traeger for 15 minutes while the lid is closed.
7. Add the chicken wings and Serrano chili peppers on the grill.
8. Grill for 5 minutes per side.
9. Remove chili peppers and place in a food processor.
10. Grill the chicken for another 20 minutes.
11. Add the rest of the ingredients to the food processor.
12. Pulse until smooth.
13. Dip the chicken wings in the sauce.
14. Grill for 5 minutes and serve.

Budget Friendly Chicken Legs

Servings: 6

Cooking Time: 1½ Hours

Ingredients:

- For Brine:
- 1 C. kosher salt
- ¾ C. light brown sugar
- 16 C. water
- 6 chicken leg quarters
- For Glaze:
- ½ C. mayonnaise
- 2 tbsp. BBQ rub
- 2 tbsp. fresh chives, minced
- 1 tbsp. garlic, minced

Directions:

1. For brine: in a bucket, dissolve salt and brown sugar in water.
2. Place the chicken quarters in brine and refrigerate, covered for about 4 hours.
3. When ready to cook, turn the Traeger on and set the temperature to 275°F and preheat with closed lid for 15 minutes.
4. Remove chicken quarters from brine and rinse under cold running water.
5. With paper towels, pat dry chicken quarters.
6. For glaze: in a bowl, add all ingredients and mix till ell combined.
7. Coat chicken quarters with glaze evenly.
8. Place the chicken leg quarters onto grill and cook for about 1-1½ hours.
9. Serve immediately.

Wood Pellet Grilled Chicken

Servings: 6

Cooking Time: 1 Hours And 10 Minutes

Ingredients:

- 5 pounds whole chicken
- 1/2 cup oil
- Chicken rub

Directions:

1. When ready to cook, turn the Traeger on and set the temperature to 400°F. Preheat your Traeger on smoke with the lid open for 5 minutes. Close the lid, increase the temperature to 450°F and preheat for 15 more minutes.
2. Tie the chicken legs together with the baker's twine then rub the chicken with oil and coat with chicken rub.
3. Place the chicken on the grill with the breast side up.
4. Grill the chicken for 70 minutes without opening it or until the internal temperature reaches 165°F.
5. Once the chicken is out of the grill let it cool down for 15 minutes
6. Enjoy.

Bbq Half Chickens

Servings: 4

Cooking Time: 75 Minutes

Ingredients:

- 3.5-pound whole chicken, cleaned, halved
- Summer rub as needed
- Apricot BBQ sauce as needed

Directions:

1. When ready to cook, turn the Traeger on and set the temperature to 375°F and let it preheat for a minimum of 15 minutes.
2. Meanwhile, cut chicken in half along with backbone and then season with summer rub.
3. When the grill has preheated, open the lid, place chicken halves on the grill grate skin-side up, shut the grill, change the smoking temperature to 225°F, and smoke for 1 hours and 30 minutes until the internal temperature reaches 160°F.
4. Then brush chicken generously with apricot sauce and continue grilling for 10 minutes until glazed.
5. When done, transfer chicken to cutting to a dish, let it rest for 5 minutes, and then serve.

Buffalo Chicken Flatbread

Servings: 6

Cooking Time: 30 Minutes

Ingredients:

- 6 mini pita bread
- 1-1/2 cups buffalo sauce
- 4 cups chicken breasts, cooked and cubed
- 3 cups mozzarella cheese
- Blue cheese for drizzling

Directions:

1. When ready to cook, turn the Traeger on and set the temperature to 375°F.
2. Place the breads on a flat surface and evenly spread sauce over all of them.
3. Toss the chicken with the remaining buffalo sauce and place it on the pita breads.
4. Top with cheese then place the breads on the grill but indirectly from the heat. Close the grill lid.
5. Cook for 7 minutes or until the cheese has melted and the edges are toasty.
6. Remove from grill and drizzle with blue cheese. Serve and enjoy.

Sweet Sriracha Bbq Chicken

👥 **Servings: 5**

🕐 **Cooking Time: 1 And ½-2 Hours**

Ingredients:

- 1cup sriracha
- ½ cup butter
- ½ cup molasses
- ½ cup ketchup
- ¼ cup firmly packed brown sugar
- 1teaspoon salt
- 1teaspoon fresh ground black pepper
- 1whole chicken, cut into pieces
- ½ teaspoon fresh parsley leaves, chopped

Directions:

1. When ready to cook, turn the Traeger on and set the temperature to 250°F using cherry wood.
2. Take a medium saucepan and place it over low heat, stir in butter, sriracha, ketchup, molasses, brown sugar, mustard, pepper and salt and keep stirring until the sugar and salt dissolves.
3. Divide the sauce into two portions.
4. Brush the chicken half with the sauce and reserve the remaining for serving.
5. Make sure to keep the sauce for serving on the side, and keep the other portion for basting.
6. Transfer chicken to your smoker rack and smoke for about 1 and a ½ to 2 hours until the internal temperature reaches 165°F.
7. Sprinkle chicken with parsley and serve with reserved BBQ sauce.

Enjoy!

Wood Pellet Smoked Spatchcock Turkey

👥 **Servings: 6**

🕐 **Cooking Time: 1 Hours 45 Minutes**

Ingredients:

- 1 whole turkey
- 1/2 cup oil
- 1/4 cup chicken rub
- 1 tbsp onion powder
- 1 tbsp garlic powder
- 1 tbsp rubbed sage

Directions:

1. When ready to cook, turn the Traeger on and set the temperature to High.
2. Meanwhile, place the turkey on a platter with the breast side down then cut on either side of the backbone to remove the spine.
3. Flip the turkey and season on both sides then place it on the preheated grill or on a pan if you want to catch the drippings.
4. Grill on high for 30 minutes, reduce the temperature to 325°F, and grill for 45 more minutes or until the internal temperature reaches 165°F
5. Remove from the grill and let rest for 20 minutes before slicing and serving. Enjoy.

Cinco De Mayo Chicken Enchiladas

Servings: 6

Cooking Time: 45 Minutes

Ingredients:

- 6 cups diced cooked chicken
- 3 cups grated Monterey Jack cheese, divided
- 1 cup sour cream
- 1 (4-ounce) can chopped green chiles
- 2 (10-ounce) cans red or green enchilada sauce, divided
- 12 (8-inch) flour tortillas
- ½ cup chopped scallions
- ¼ cup chopped fresh cilantro

Directions:

1. When ready to cook, turn the Traeger on and set the temperature to 350°F. Preheat with the lid closed.
2. In a large bowl, combine the cooked chicken, 2 cups of cheese, the sour cream, and green chiles to make the filling.
3. Pour one can of enchilada sauce in the bottom of a 9-by-13-inch baking dish or aluminum pan.
4. Spoon ⅓ cup of the filling on each tortilla and roll up securely.
5. Transfer the tortillas seam-side down to the baking dish, then pour the remaining can of enchilada sauce over them, coating all exposed surfaces of the tortillas.
6. Sprinkle the remaining 1 cup of cheese over the enchiladas and cover tightly with aluminum foil.
7. Bake on the grill, with the lid closed, for 30 minutes, then remove the foil.
8. Continue baking with the lid closed for 15 minutes, or until bubbly.
9. Garnish the enchiladas with the chopped scallions and cilantro and serve immediately.

Spatchcocked Turkey

Servings: 10 To 14

Cooking Time: 2 Hours

Ingredients:

- 1 whole turkey
- 2 tablespoons olive oil
- 1 batch Chicken Rub

Directions:

1. When ready to cook, turn the Traeger on and set the temperature to 350°F. Preheat the grill with the lid closed.
2. To remove the turkey's backbone, place the turkey on a work surface, on its breast. Using kitchen shears, cut along one side of the turkey's backbone and then the other. Pull out the bone.
3. Once the backbone is removed, turn the turkey breast-side up and flatten it.
4. Coat the turkey with olive oil and season it on both sides with the rub. Using your hands, work the rub into the meat and skin.
5. Place the turkey directly on the grill grate, breast-side up, and cook until its internal temperature reaches 170°F.
6. Remove the turkey from the grill and let it rest for 10 minutes, before carving and serving.

Wood Pellet Chile Lime Chicken

Servings: 1

Cooking Time: 15 Minutes

Ingredients:

- 1 chicken breast
- 1 tbsp oil
- 1 tbsp chile-lime seasoning

Directions:

1. When ready to cook, turn the Traeger on and set the temperature to 400°F.
2. Brush the chicken breast with oil on all sides.
3. Sprinkle with seasoning and salt to taste.
4. Grill for 7 minutes per side or until the internal temperature reaches 165°F.
5. Serve when hot or cold and enjoy.

Buffalo Chicken Wraps

Servings: 4

Cooking Time: 20 Minutes

Ingredients:

- 2 teaspoons poultry seasoning
- 1 teaspoon freshly ground black pepper
- 1 teaspoon garlic powder
- 1 to 1½ pounds chicken tenders
- 4 tablespoons (½ stick) unsalted butter, melted
- ½ cup hot sauce (such as Frank's RedHot)
- 4 (10-inch) flour tortillas
- 1 cup shredded lettuce
- ½ cup diced tomato
- ½ cup diced celery
- ½ cup diced red onion
- ½ cup shredded Cheddar cheese
- ¼ cup blue cheese crumbles
- ¼ cup prepared ranch dressing
- 2 tablespoons sliced pickled jalapeño peppers (optional)

Directions:

1. When ready to cook, turn the Traeger on and set the temperature to 350°F. Preheat with the lid closed.
2. In a small bowl, stir together the poultry seasoning, pepper, and garlic powder to create an all-purpose rub, and season the chicken tenders with it.
3. Arrange the tenders directly on the grill, close the lid, and smoke for 20 minutes, or until a meat thermometer inserted in the thickest part of the meat reads 170°F.
4. In another bowl, stir together the melted butter and hot sauce and coat the smoked chicken with it.
5. To serve, heat the tortillas on the grill for less than a minute on each side and place on a plate.
6. Top each tortilla with some of the lettuce, tomato, celery, red onion, Cheddar cheese, blue cheese crumbles, ranch dressing, and jalapeños (if using).
7. Divide the chicken among the tortillas, close up securely, and serve.

Jamaican Jerk Chicken Quarters

Servings: 4

Cooking Time: 1 To 2 Hours

Ingredients:

- 4 chicken leg quarters, scored
- ¼ cup canola oil
- ½ cup Jamaican Jerk Paste
- 1 tablespoon whole allspice (pimento) berries

Directions:

1. When ready to cook, turn the Traeger on and set the temperature to 275°F.
2. Brush the chicken with canola oil, then brush 6 tablespoons of the Jerk paste on and under the skin. Reserve the remaining 2 tablespoons of paste for basting.
3. Throw the whole allspice berries in with the wood pellets for added smoke flavor.
4. Arrange the chicken on the grill, close the lid, and smoke for 1 hours to 1 hours 30 minutes, or until a meat thermometer inserted in the thickest part of the thigh reads 165°F.
5. Let the meat rest for 5 minutes and baste with the reserved jerk paste prior to serving.

South-east-asian Chicken Drumsticks

Servings: 6

Cooking Time: 2 Hours

Ingredients:

- 1 C. fresh orange juice
- ¼ C. honey
- 2 tbsp. sweet chili sauce
- 2 tbsp. hoisin sauce
- 2 tbsp. fresh ginger, grated finely
- 2 tbsp. garlic, minced
- 1 tsp. Sriracha
- ½ tsp. sesame oil
- 6 chicken drumsticks

Directions:

1. When ready to cook, turn the Traeger on and set the temperature to 225°F and preheat with closed lid for 15 minutes, using charcoal.
2. In a bowl, place all ingredients except for chicken drumsticks and mix until well combined.
3. Reserve half of honey mixture in a small bowl.
4. In the bowl of remaining sauce, add drumsticks and mix well.
5. Arrange the chicken drumsticks onto the grill and cook for about 2 hours, basting with remaining sauce occasionally.
6. Serve hot.

Smoked And Fried Chicken Wings

👪 **Servings: 6**

🕐 **Cooking Time: 2 Hours**

Ingredients:

- 3 pounds chicken wings
- 1 tbsp Goya adobo all-purpose seasoning
- Sauce of your choice

Directions:

1. When ready to cook, turn the Traeger on and set the temperature to Smoke.
2. Meanwhile, coat the chicken wings with adobo all-purpose seasoning. Place the chicken on the grill and smoke for 2 hours.
3. Remove the wings from the grill.
4. Preheat oil to 375°F in a frying pan. Drop the wings in batches and let fry for 5 minutes or until the skin is crispy.
5. Drain the oil and proceed with drizzling preferred sauce
6. Drain oil and drizzle preferred sauce
7. Enjoy.

Wood Pellet Chicken Breasts

👪 **Servings: 6**

🕐 **Cooking Time: 15 Minutes**

Ingredients:

- 3 chicken breasts
- 1 tbsp avocado oil
- 1/4 tbsp garlic powder
- 1/4 tbsp onion powder
- 3/4 tbsp salt
- 1/4 tbsp pepper

Directions:

1. When ready to cook, turn the Traeger on and set the temperature to 375°F.
2. Half the chicken breasts lengthwise then coat with avocado oil.
3. With the spices, drizzle it on all sides to season.
4. Drizzle spices to season the chicken. Put the chicken on top of the grill and begin to cook until its internal temperature approaches 165°F. Put the chicken on top of the grill and begin to cook until it rises to a temperature of 165°F.
5. Serve and enjoy.

Bacon-wrapped Chicken Tenders

Servings: 6

Cooking Time: 30 Minutes

Ingredients:

- 1-pound chicken tenders
- 10 strips bacon
- 1/2 tbsp Italian seasoning
- 1/2 tbsp black pepper
- 1/2 tbsp salt
- 1 tbsp paprika
- 1 tbsp onion powder
- 1 tbsp garlic powder
- 1/3 cup light brown sugar
- 1 tbsp chili powder

Directions:

1. When ready to cook, turn the Traeger on and set the temperature to 350°F.
2. Mix seasonings
3. Sprinkle the mixture on all sides of chicken tenders
4. Wrap each chicken tender with a strip of bacon
5. Mix sugar and chili then sprinkle the mixture on the bacon-wrapped chicken.
6. Place them on the smoker and smoker for 30 minutes with the lid closed or until the chicken is cooked.
7. Serve and enjoy.

Wood Pellet Grilled Buffalo Chicken Leg

Servings: 6

Cooking Time: 25 Minutes

Ingredients:

- 12 chicken legs
- 1/2 tbsp salt
- 1 tbsp buffalo seasoning
- 1 cup buffalo sauce

Directions:

1. When ready to cook, turn the Traeger on and set the temperature to 325°F.
2. Toss the legs in salt and buffalo seasoning then place them on the preheated grill.
3. Grill for 40 minutes ensuring you turn them twice through the cooking.
4. Brush the legs with buffalo sauce and cook for an additional 10 minutes or until the internal temperature reaches 165°F.
5. Remove the legs from the grill, brush with more sauce, and serve when hot.

Wood Pellet Grilled Buffalo Chicken

👪 **Servings: 6**

🕐 **Cooking Time: 20 Minutes**

Ingredients:

- 5 chicken breasts, boneless and skinless
- 2 tbsp homemade barbeque rub
- 1 cup homemade Cholula buffalo sauce

Directions:

1. When ready to cook, turn the Traeger on and set the temperature to 400°F.
2. Slice the chicken into long strips and season with barbeque rub.
3. Place the chicken on the grill and paint both sides with buffalo sauce.
4. Cook for 4 minutes with the grill closed. Cook while flipping and painting with buffalo sauce every 5 minutes until the internal temperature reaches 165°F.
5. Remove from the grill and serve when warm. Enjoy.

Smoked Turkey Wings

👪 **Servings: 2**

🕐 **Cooking Time: 1 Hours**

Ingredients:

- 4 turkey wings
- 1 batch Sweet and Spicy Cinnamon Rub

Directions:

1. When ready to cook, turn the Traeger on and set the temperature to 180°F. Preheat the grill with the lid closed.
2. Using your hands, work the rub into the turkey wings, coating them completely.
3. Place the wings directly on the grill grate and cook for 30 minutes.
4. Increase the grill's temperature to 325°F and continue to cook until the turkey's internal temperature reaches 170°F. Remove the wings from the grill and serve immediately.

Smoked Whole Chicken

👥 **Servings: 6 To 8**

🕐 **Cooking Time: 4 Hours**

Ingredients:

- 1 whole chicken
- 2 cups Tea Injectable (using Not-Just-for-Pork Rub)
- 2 tablespoons olive oil
- 1 batch Chicken Rub
- 2 tablespoons butter, melted

Directions:

1. When ready to cook, turn the Traeger on and set the temperature to 180°F. Preheat the grill with the lid closed.
2. Inject the chicken throughout with the tea injectable.
3. Coat the chicken all over with olive oil and season it with the rub. Using your hands, work the rub into the meat.
4. Place the chicken directly on the grill grate and smoke for 3 hours.
5. Baste the chicken with the butter and increase the grill's temperature to 375°F. Continue to cook the chicken until its internal temperature reaches 170°F.
6. Remove the chicken from the grill and let it rest for 10 minutes, before carving and serving.

Herb Roasted Turkey

👥 **Servings: 12**

🕐 **Cooking Time: 3 Hours And 30 Minutes**

Ingredients:

- 14 pounds turkey, cleaned
- 2 tablespoons chopped mixed herbs
- Pork and poultry rub as needed
- 1/4 teaspoon ground black pepper
- 3 tablespoons butter, unsalted, melted
- 8 tablespoons butter, unsalted, softened
- 2 cups chicken broth
-

Directions:

1. Clean the turkey by removing the giblets, wash it inside out, pat dry with paper towels, then place it on a roasting pan and tuck the turkey wings by tiring with butcher's string.
2. When ready to cook, turn the Traeger on and set the temperature to 325°F and let it preheat for a minimum of 15 minutes.
3. Meanwhile, prepared herb butter and for this, take a small bowl, place the softened butter in it, add black pepper and mixed herbs and beat until fluffy.
4. Place some of the prepared herb butter underneath the skin of turkey by using a handle of a wooden spoon, and massage the skin to distribute butter evenly.
5. Then rub the exterior of the turkey with melted butter, season with pork and poultry rub, and pour the broth in the roasting pan.
6. When the grill has preheated, open the lid, place roasting pan containing turkey on the grill grate, shut the grill and smoke for 3 hours and 30 minutes until the internal temperature reaches 165°F and the top has turned golden brown.
7. When done, transfer turkey to a cutting board, let it rest for 30 minutes, then carve it into slices and serve.

Skinny Smoked Chicken Breasts

Servings: 4 To 6

Cooking Time: 1 Hours 25 Minutes

Ingredients:

- 2½ pounds boneless, skinless chicken breasts
- Salt
- Freshly ground black pepper

Directions:

1. When ready to cook, turn the Traeger on and set the temperature to 180°F. Preheat the grill with the lid closed.
2. Season the chicken breasts all over with salt and pepper.
3. Place the breasts directly on the grill grate and smoke for 1 hours.
4. Increase the grill's temperature to 325°F and continue to cook until the chicken's internal temperature reaches 170°F. Remove the breasts from the grill and serve immediately.

Cajun Chicken

Servings: 4

Cooking Time: 30 Minutes

Ingredients:

- 2 lb. chicken wings
- Poultry dry rub
- Cajun seasoning

Directions:

1. Season the chicken wings with the dry rub and Cajun seasoning.
2. When ready to cook, turn the Traeger on and set the temperature to 350°F. Preheat the Traeger to 350°F for 15 minutes while the lid is closed.
3. Grill for 30 minutes, flipping twice.

Smoked Turkey Breast

👥 **Servings: 2 To 4**

🕐 **Cooking Time: 1 To 2 Hours**

Ingredients:

- 1 (3-pound) turkey breast
- Salt
- Freshly ground black pepper
- 1 teaspoon garlic powder

Directions:

1. When ready to cook, turn the Traeger on and set the temperature to 180°F. Preheat the grill with the lid closed.
2. Season the turkey breast all over with salt, pepper, and garlic powder.
3. Place the breast directly on the grill grate and smoke for 1 hours.
4. Increase the grill's temperature to 350°F and continue to cook until the turkey's internal temperature reaches 170°F. Remove the breast from the grill and serve immediately.

Ultimate Tasty Chicken

👥 **Servings: 5**

🕐 **Cooking Time: 3 Hours**

Ingredients:

- For Brine:
- 1 C. brown sugar
- ½ C. kosher salt
- 16 C. water
- For Chicken:
- 1 (3-lb.) whole chicken
- 1 tbsp. garlic, crushed
- 1 tsp. onion powder
- Salt and freshly ground black pepper, to taste
- 1 medium yellow onion, quartered
- 3 whole garlic cloves, peeled
- 1 lemon, quartered
- 4-5 fresh thyme sprigs

Directions:

1. For brine: in a bucket, dissolve brown sugar and kosher salt in water.
2. Place the chicken in brine and refrigerate overnight.
3. When ready to cook, turn the Traeger on and set the temperature to 225°F and preheat with closed lid for 15 minutes.
4. Remove the chicken from brine and with paper towels, pat it dry.
5. In a small bowl, mix together crushed garlic, onion powder, salt and black pepper.
6. Rub the chicken with garlic mixture evenly.
7. Stuff the cavity of chicken with onion, garlic cloves, lemon and thyme.
8. With kitchen strings, tie the legs together.
9. Place the chicken onto grill and cook, covered for about 2½-3 hours.
10. Remove chicken from pallet grill and transfer onto a cutting board for about 10 minutes before carving.
11. With a sharp knife, cut the chicken in desired sized pieces and serve.

Thanksgiving Dinner Turkey

👪 Servings: 16

🕐 Cooking Time: 4 Hours

Ingredients:

- ½ lb. butter, softened
- 2 tbsp. fresh thyme, chopped
- 2 tbsp. fresh rosemary, chopped
- 6 garlic cloves, crushed
- 1 (20-lb.) whole turkey, neck and giblets removed
- Salt and freshly ground black pepper, to taste

Directions:

When ready to cook, turn the Traeger on and set the temperature to 300°F and preheat with closed lid for 15 minutes, using charcoal.
In a bowl, place butter, fresh herbs, garlic, salt and black pepper and mix well.
With your fingers, separate the turkey skin from breast to create a pocket.
Stuff the breast pocket with ¼-inch thick layer of butter mixture.
Season the turkey with salt and black pepper evenly.
Arrange the turkey onto the grill and cook for 3-4 hours.
Remove the turkey from grill and place onto a cutting board for about 15-20 minutes before carving.
With a sharp knife, cut the turkey into desired-sized pieces and serve.

Chinese Inspired Duck Legs

👪 Servings: 8

🕐 Cooking Time: 1 Hours 10 Minutes

Ingredients:

- For Glaze:
- ¼ C. fresh orange juice
- ¼ C. orange marmalade
- ¼ C. mirin
- 2 tbsp. hoisin sauce
- ½ tsp. red pepper flakes, crushed
- For Duck:
- 1 tsp. kosher salt
- ¾ tsp. freshly ground black pepper
- ¾ tsp. Chinese five-spice powder
- 8 (6-oz.) duck legs

Directions:

1. When ready to cook, turn the Traeger on and set the temperature to 235°F and preheat with closed lid for 15 minutes.
2. Forb glaze: in a small pan, add all ingredients over medium-high heat and bring to gentle boil, stirring continuously.
3. Remove from heat and set aside.
4. For rub: in a small bowl, mix together salt, black pepper and five-spice powder.
5. Rub the duck legs with spice rub evenly.
6. Place the duck legs onto the grill, skin side up and cook for about 50 minutes.
7. Coat the duck legs with glaze ad cook for about 20 minutes, flipping and coating with glaze after every 5 minutes.

Barbecue Chicken Wings

👥 **Servings: 4**

🕐 **Cooking Time: 15 Minutes**

Ingredients:

- Fresh chicken wings
- Salt to taste
- Pepper to taste
- Garlic powder
- Onion powder
- Cayenne
- Paprika
- Seasoning salt
- Bbq sauce to taste

Directions:

1. When ready to cook, turn the Traeger on and set the temperature to low.
2. In a mixing bowl, mix all the seasoning ingredients then toss the chicken wings until well coated.
3. Place the wings on the grill and cook for 20 minutes or until the wings are fully cooked.
4. Let rest to cool for 5 minutes then toss with bbq sauce.
5. Serve with orzo and salad. Enjoy.

Wood-fired Chicken Breasts

👥 **Servings: 2 To 4**

🕐 **Cooking Time: 45 Minutes**

Ingredients:

- 2 (1-pound) bone-in, skin-on chicken breasts
- 1 batch Chicken Rub

Directions:

1. When ready to cook, turn the Traeger on and set the temperature to 350°F. Preheat the grill with the lid closed.
2. Season the chicken breasts all over with the rub. Using your hands, work the rub into the meat.
3. Place the breasts directly on the grill grate and smoke until their internal temperature reaches 170°F. Remove the breasts from the grill and serve immediately.

Smoking Duck With Mandarin Glaze

👥 **Servings: 4**

🕐 **Cooking Time: 4 Hours**

Ingredients:

- 1 quart buttermilk
- 1 (5-pound) whole duck
- ¾ cup soy sauce
- ½ cup hoisin sauce
- ½ cup rice wine vinegar
- 2 tablespoons sesame oil
- 1 tablespoon freshly ground black pepper
- 1 tablespoon minced garlic
- Mandarin Glaze, for drizzling

Directions:

1. With a very sharp knife, remove as much fat from the duck as you can. Refrigerate or freeze the fat for later use.
2. Pour the buttermilk into a large container with a lid and submerge the whole duck in it. Cover and let brine in the refrigerator for 4 to 6 hours.
3. When ready to cook, turn the Traeger on and set the temperature to 250°F. Preheat with the lid closed.
4. Remove the duck from the buttermilk brine, then rinse it and pat dry with paper towels.
5. In a bowl, combine the soy sauce, hoisin sauce, vinegar, sesame oil, pepper, and garlic to form a paste. Reserve ¼ cup for basting.
6. Poke holes in the skin of the duck and rub the remaining paste all over and inside the cavity.
7. Place the duck on the grill breast-side down, close the lid, and smoke for about 4 hours, basting every hours with the reserved paste, until a meat thermometer inserted in the thickest part of the meat reads 165°F. Use aluminum foil to tent the duck in the last 30 minutes or so if it starts to brown too quickly.
8. To finish, drizzle with glaze.

Sweet And Spicy Smoked Wings

👥 **Servings: 2 To 4**

🕐 **Cooking Time: 1 Hours, 25 Minutes**

Ingredients:

- 1 pound chicken wings
- 1 batch Sweet and Spicy Cinnamon Rub
- 1 cup barbecue sauce

Directions:

1. When ready to cook, turn the Traeger on and set the temperature to 325°F. Preheat the grill with the lid closed.
2. Season the chicken wings with the rub. Using your hands, work the rub into the meat.
3. Place the wings directly on the grill grate and cook until they reach an internal temperature of 165°F.
4. Transfer the wings into an aluminum pan. Add the barbecue sauce and stir to coat the wings.
5. Reduce the grill's temperature to 250°F and put the pan on the grill. Smoke the wings for 1 hours more, uncovered. Remove the wings from the grill and serve immediately.

Smoked Fried Chicken

👪 Servings: 6

🕐 Cooking Time: 3 Hours

Ingredients:

- 3.5 lb. chicken
- Vegetable oil
- Salt and pepper to taste
- 2 tablespoons hot sauce
- 1 quart buttermilk
- 2 tablespoons brown sugar
- 1 tablespoon poultry dry rub
- 2 tablespoons onion powder
- 2 tablespoons garlic powder
- 2 1/2 cups all-purpose flour
- Peanut oil

Directions:

1. When ready to cook, turn the Traeger on and set the temperature to 200°F.
2. Preheat it for 15 minutes while the lid is closed.
3. Drizzle chicken with vegetable oil and sprinkle with salt and pepper.
4. Smoke chicken for 2 hours and 30 minutes.
5. In a bowl, mix the hot sauce, buttermilk and sugar.
6. Soak the smoked chicken in the mixture.
7. Cover and refrigerate for 1 hours.
8. In another bowl, mix the dry rub, onion powder, garlic powder and flour.
9. Coat the chicken with the mixture.
10. Heat the peanut oil in a pan over medium heat.
11. Fry the chicken until golden and crispy.

Wood Pellet Smoked Cornish Hens

👪 Servings: 6

🕐 Cooking Time: 1 Hours

Ingredients:

6 Cornish hens

3 tbsp avocado oil

6 tbsp rub of choice

Directions:

1. When ready to cook, turn the Traeger on and set the temperature to 275°F.
2. Rub the hens with oil then coat generously with rub. Place the hens on the grill with the chest breast side down.
3. Smoke for 30 minutes. Flip the hens and increase the grill temperature to 400°F. Cook until the internal temperature reaches 165°F.
4. Remove from the grill and let rest for 10 minutes before serving. Enjoy.

Maple And Bacon Chicken

Servings: 7

Cooking Time: 1 And ½ Hours

Ingredients:

- 4 boneless and skinless chicken breast
- Salt as needed
- Fresh pepper
- 12 slices bacon, uncooked
- 1cup maple syrup
- ½ cup melted butter
- 1teaspoon liquid smoke

Directions:

1. When ready to cook, turn the Traeger on and set the temperature to 250°F.
2. Season the chicken with pepper and salt.
3. Wrap the breast with 3 bacon slices and cover the entire surface.
4. Secure the bacon with toothpicks.
5. Take a medium-sized bowl and stir in maple syrup, butter, liquid smoke, and mix well.
6. Reserve 1/3rd of this mixture for later use.
7. Submerge the chicken breast into the butter mix and coat them well.
8. Place a pan in your smoker and transfer the chicken to your smoker.
9. Smoker for 1 to 1 and a ½ hours.
10. Brush the chicken with reserved butter and smoke for 30 minutes more until the internal temperature reaches 165°F.
11. Enjoy!

4

Fish And Seafood Recipes

Blackened Catfish

👪 **Servings: 4**

🕐 **Cooking Time: 40 Minutes**

Ingredients:

- Spice blend
- 1 teaspoon granulated garlic
- 1/4 teaspoon cayenne pepper
- 1/2 cup Cajun seasoning
- 1 teaspoon ground thyme
- 1 teaspoon ground oregano
- 1 teaspoon onion powder
- 1 tablespoon smoked paprika
- 1 teaspoon pepper
- Fish
- 4 catfish fillets
- Salt to taste
- 1/2 cup butter

Directions:

1. In a bowl, combine all the ingredients for the spice blend.
2. Sprinkle both sides of the fish with the salt and spice blend.
3. When ready to cook, turn the Traeger on and set the temperature to 450°F.
4. Heat your cast iron pan and add the butter. Add the fillets to the pan.
5. Cook for 5 minutes per side.
6. Serving Suggestion: Garnish with lemon wedges.

Lively Flavored Shrimp

👪 **Servings: 6**

🕐 **Cooking Time: 30 Minutes**

Ingredients:

- 8 oz. salted butter, melted
- ¼ C. Worcestershire sauce
- ¼ C. fresh parsley, chopped
- 1 lemon, quartered
- 2 lb. jumbo shrimp, peeled and deveined
- 3 tbsp. BBQ rub

Directions:

1. In a metal baking pan, add all ingredients except for shrimp and BBQ rub and mix well.
2. Season the shrimp with BBQ rub evenly.
3. Add the shrimp in the pan with butter mixture and coat well.
4. Set aside for about 20-30 minutes.
5. When ready to cook, turn the Traeger on and set the temperature to 250°F and preheat with closed lid for 15 minutes.
6. Place the pan onto the grill and cook for about 25-30 minutes.
7. Remove the pan from grill and serve hot.

Flavor-bursting Prawn Skewers

Servings: 5

Cooking Time: 8 Minutes

Ingredients:

- ¼ C. fresh parsley leaves, minced
- 1 tbsp. garlic, crushed
- 2½ tbsp. olive oil
- 2 tbsp. Thai chili sauce
- 1 tbsp. fresh lime juice
- 1½ pounds prawns, peeled and deveined

Directions:

1. In a large bowl, add all ingredients except for prawns and mix well.
2. In a resealable plastic bag, add marinade and prawns.
3. Seal the bag and shake to coat well
4. Refrigerate for about 20-30 minutes.
5. When ready to cook, turn the Traeger on and set the temperature to 450°F and preheat with closed lid for 15 minutes.
6. Remove the prawns from marinade and thread onto metal skewers.
7. Arrange the skewers onto the grill and cook for about 4 minutes per side.

Remove the skewers from grill and serve hot.

Lemon Garlic Scallops

Servings: 6

Cooking Time: 5 Minutes

Ingredients:

- 1 dozen scallops
- 2 tablespoons chopped parsley
- Salt as needed
- 1 tablespoon olive oil
- 1 tablespoon butter, unsalted
- 1 teaspoon lemon zest
- For the Garlic Butter:
- ½ teaspoon minced garlic
- 1 lemon, juiced
- 4 tablespoons butter, unsalted, melted

Directions:

1. When ready to cook, turn the Traeger on and set the temperature to 400°F and let it preheat for a minimum of 15 minutes.
2. Meanwhile, remove frill from scallops, pat dry with paper towels and then season with salt and black pepper.
3. When the grill has preheated, open the lid, place a skillet on the grill grate, add butter and oil, and when the butter melts, place seasoned scallops on it and then cook for 2 minutes until seared.
4. Meanwhile, prepare the garlic butter and for this, take a small bowl, place all of its ingredients in it and then whisk until combined.
5. Flip the scallops, top with some of the prepared garlic butter, and cook for another minute.
6. When done, transfer scallops to a dish, top with remaining garlic butter, sprinkle with parsley and lemon zest, and then serve.

Citrus-smoked Trout

👥 **Servings: 6**

🕐 **Cooking Time: 1 To 2 Hours**

Ingredients:

- 6 to 8 skin-on rainbow trout, cleaned and scaled
- 1 gallon orange juice
- ½ cup packed light brown sugar
- ¼ cup salt
- 1 tablespoon freshly ground black pepper
- Nonstick spray, oil, or butter, for greasing
- 1 tablespoon chopped fresh parsley
- 1 lemon, sliced

Directions:

1. Fillet the fish and pat dry with paper towels.
2. Pour the orange juice into a large container with a lid and stir in the brown sugar, salt, and pepper.
3. Place the trout in the brine, cover, and refrigerate for 1 hours.
4. Cover the grill grate with heavy-duty aluminum foil. Poke holes in the foil and spray with cooking spray .
5. When ready to cook, turn the Traeger on and set the temperature to 225°F. Preheat with the lid closed.
6. Remove the trout from the brine and pat dry. Arrange the fish on the foil-covered grill grate, close the lid, and smoke for 1 hours 30 minutes to 2 hours, or until flaky.
7. Remove the fish from the heat. Serve garnished with the fresh parsley and lemon slices.

Smoked Scallops

👥 **Servings: 6**

🕐 **Cooking Time: 15 Minutes**

Ingredients:

- 2 pounds sea scallops
- 4 tbsp salted butter
- 2 tbsp lemon juice
- ½ tsp ground black pepper
- 1 garlic clove (minced)
- 1 kosher tsp salt
- 1 tsp freshly chopped tarragon

Directions:

1. Let the scallops dry using paper towels and drizzle all sides with salt and pepper to season
2. When ready to cook, turn the Traeger on and set the temperature to 400°F preheat the grill with lid closed for 15 minutes.
3. Combine the butter and garlic in hot cast iron pan. Add the scallops and stir. Close grill lid and cook for 8 minutes. Flip the scallops and cook for an additional 7 minutes.
4. Remove the scallop from heat and let it rest for a few minutes.
5. Stir in the chopped tarragon. Serve and top with lemon juice.

Wine Infused Salmon

👬 **Servings: 4**

🕐 **Cooking Time: 5 Hours**

Ingredients:

- 2 C. low-sodium soy sauce
- 1 C. dry white wine
- 1 C. water
- ½ tsp. Tabasco sauce
- 1/3 C. sugar
- ¼ C. salt
- ½ tsp. garlic powder
- ½ tsp. onion powder
- Freshly ground black pepper, to taste
- 4 (6-oz.) salmon fillets

Directions:

1. In a large bowl, add all ingredients except salmon and stir until sugar is dissolved.
2. Add salmon fillets and coat with brine well.
3. Refrigerate, covered overnight.
4. Remove salmon from bowl and rinse under cold running water.
5. With paper towels, pat dry the salmon fillets.
6. Arrange a wire rack in a sheet pan.
7. Place the salmon fillets onto wire rack, skin side down and set aside to cool for about 1 hours.
8. When ready to cook, turn the Traeger on and set the temperature to 165°F and preheat with closed lid for 15 minutes, using charcoal.
9. Place the salmon fillets onto the grill, skin side down and cook for about 3-5 hours or until desired doneness.
10. Remove the salmon fillets from grill and serve hot.

Oysters In The Shell

👬 **Servings: 4**

🕐 **Cooking Time: 20 Minutes**

Ingredients:

- 8 medium oysters, unopened, in the shell, rinsed and scrubbed
- 1 batch Lemon Butter Mop for Seafood

Directions:

1. When ready to cook, turn the Traeger on and set the temperature to 375°F. Preheat the grill with the lid closed.
2. Place the unopened oysters directly on the grill grate and grill for about 20 minutes, or until the oysters are done and their shells open.
3. Discard any oysters that do not open. Shuck the remaining oysters, transfer them to a bowl, and add the mop. Serve immediately.

Grilled Tilapia

👪 **Servings: 6**

🕐 **Cooking Time: 2o Minutes**

Ingredients:

- 2 tsp dried parsley
- ½ tsp garlic powder
- 1 tsp cayenne pepper
- ½ tsp ground black pepper
- ½ tsp thyme
- ½ tsp dried basil
- ½ tsp oregano
- 3 tbsp olive oil
- ½ tsp lemon pepper
- 1 tsp kosher salt
- 1 lemon (juiced)
- 6 tilapia fillets
- 1 ½ tsp creole seafood seasoning

Directions:

1. In a mixing bowl, combine spices
2. Brush the fillets with oil and lemon juice.
3. Liberally, season all sides of the tilapia fillets with the seasoning mix.
4. Preheat your grill to 325°F
5. Place a non-stick BBQ grilling try on the grill and arrange the tilapia fillets onto it.
6. Grill for 15 to 20 minutes
7. Remove fillets and cool down

Grilled Tuna

👪 **Servings: 4**

🕐 **Cooking Time: 4 Minutes**

Ingredients:

- 4 (6 ounce each) tuna steaks (1 inch thick)
- 1 lemon (juiced)
- 1 clove garlic (minced)
- 1 tsp chili
- 2 tbsp extra virgin olive oil
- 1 cup white wine
- 3 tbsp brown sugar
- 1 tsp rosemary

Directions:

1. Combine lemon, chili, white wine, sugar, rosemary, olive oil and garlic. Add the tuna steaks and toss to combine.
2. Transfer the tuna and marinade to a zip-lock bag. Refrigerate for 3 hours.
3. Remove the tuna steaks from the marinade and let them rest for about 1 hours
4. When ready to cook, turn the Traeger on and set to smoke, leaving the lid opened for 5 minutes, or until fire starts.
5. Do not open lid to preheat until 15 minutes to the setting "HIGH"
6. Grease the grill grate with oil and place the tuna on the grill grate. Grill tuna steaks for 4 minutes, 2 minutes per side.
7. Remove the tuna from the grill and let them rest for a few minutes.

Super-tasty Trout

Servings: 8

Cooking Time: 5 Hours

Ingredients:

- 1 (7-lb.) whole lake trout, butterflied
- ½ C. kosher salt
- ½ C.fresh rosemary, chopped
- 2 tsp. lemon zest, grated finely

Directions:

1. Rub the trout with salt generously and then, sprinkle with rosemary and lemon zest.
2. Arrange the trout in a large baking dish and refrigerate for about 7-8 hours.
3. Remove the trout from baking dish and rinse under cold running water to remove the salt.
4. With paper towels, pat dry the trout completely.
5. Arrange a wire rack in a sheet pan.
6. Place the trout onto the wire rack, skin side down and refrigerate for about 24 hours.
7. When ready to cook, turn the Traeger on and set the temperature to 180°F and preheat with closed lid for 15 minutes, using charcoal.
8. Place the trout onto the grill and cook for about 2-4 hours or until desired doneness.
9. Remove the trout from grill and place onto a cutting board for about 5 minutes before serving.

Sriracha Salmon

Servings: 4

Cooking Time: 25 Minutes

Ingredients:

- 3-pound salmon, skin on
- For the Marinade:
- 1 teaspoon lime zest
- 1 tablespoon minced garlic
- 1 tablespoon grated ginger
- Sea salt as needed
- Ground black pepper as needed
- 1/4 cup maple syrup
- 2 tablespoons soy sauce
- 2 tablespoons Sriracha sauce
- 1 tablespoon toasted sesame oil
- 1 tablespoon rice vinegar
- 1 teaspoon toasted sesame seeds

Directions:

1. Prepare the marinade and for this, take a small bowl, place all of its ingredients in it, stir until well combined, and then pour the mixture into a large plastic bag.
2. Add salmon in the bag, seal it, turn it upside down to coat salmon with the marinade and let it marinate for a minimum of 2 hours in the refrigerator.
3. When ready to cook, turn the Traeger on and set the temperature to 450°F and let it preheat for a minimum of 5 minutes.
4. Meanwhile, take a large baking sheet, line it with parchment paper, place salmon on it skin-side down and then brush with the marinade.
5. When the grill has preheated, open the lid, place baking sheet containing salmon on the grill grate, shut the grill and smoke for 25 minutes until thoroughly cooked.
6. When done, transfer salmon to a dish and then serve.

Grilled Lingcod

👪 **Servings: 6**

🕐 **Cooking Time: 15 Minutes**

Ingredients:

- 2 lb lingcod fillets
- 1/2 tbsp salt
- 1/2 tbsp white pepper
- 1/4 tbsp cayenne
- Lemon wedges

Directions:

1. When ready to cook, turn the Traeger on and set the temperature to 375°F.
2. Place the lingcod on a parchment paper and season it with salt, white pepper, cayenne pepper then top with the lemon.
3. Place the fish on the grill and cook for 15 minutes or until the internal temperature reaches 145°F.
4. Serve and enjoy.

Cider Salmon

👪 **Servings: 4**

🕐 **Cooking Time: 1 Hours**

Ingredients:

- 1 ½ pound salmon fillet, skin-on, center-cut, pin bone removed
- For the Brine:
- 4 juniper berries, crushed
- 1 bay leaf, crumbled
- 1 piece star anise, broken
- 1 1/2 cups apple cider
- For the Cure:
- 1/2 cup salt
- 1 teaspoon ground black pepper
- 1/4 cup brown sugar
- 2 teaspoons barbecue rub

Directions:

1. Prepare the brine and for this, take a large container, add all of its ingredients in it, stir until mixed, then add salmon and let soak for a minimum of 8 hours in the refrigerator.
2. Meanwhile, prepare the cure and for this, take a small bowl, place all of its ingredients in it and stir until combined.
3. After 8 hours, remove salmon from the brine, then take a baking dish, place half of the cure in it, top with salmon skin-side down, sprinkle remaining cure on top, cover with plastic wrap and let it rest for 1 hours in the refrigerator.
4. When ready to cook, turn the Traeger on and set the temperature to 200°F and let it preheat for a minimum of 5 minutes.
5. Meanwhile, remove salmon from the cure, pat dry with paper towels, and then sprinkle with black pepper.
6. When the grill has preheated, open the lid, place salmon on the grill grate, shut the grill, and smoke for 1 hours until the internal temperature reaches 150°F.
7. When done, transfer salmon to a cutting board, let it rest for 5 minutes, then remove the skin and serve.

Teriyaki Smoked Shrimp

👪 **Servings: 6**

🕐 **Cooking Time: 20 Minutes**

Ingredients:

- Uncooked shrimp - 1 lb.
- Onion powder - ½ tbsp
- Garlic powder - ½ tbsp
- Teriyaki sauce - 4 tbsp
- Mayo - 4 tbsp
- Minced green onion - 2 tbsp
- Salt - ½ tbsp

Directions:

1. Remove the shells from the shrimp and wash thoroughly.
2. When ready to cook, turn the Traeger on and set the temperature to 450°F.
3. Season with garlic powder, onion powder, and salt.
4. Cook the shrimp for 5-6 minutes on each side.
5. Once cooked, remove the shrimp from the grill and garnish it with spring onion, teriyaki sauce, and mayo.

Jerk Shrimp

👪 **Servings: 12**

🕐 **Cooking Time: 6 Minutes**

Ingredients:

- 2 pounds shrimp, peeled, deveined
- 3 tablespoons olive oil
- For the Spice Mix:
- 1 teaspoon garlic powder
- 1 teaspoon of sea salt
- 1/4 teaspoon ground cayenne
- 1 tablespoon brown sugar
- 1/8 teaspoon smoked paprika
- 1 tablespoon smoked paprika
- 1/4 teaspoon ground thyme
- 1 lime, zested

Directions:

1. When ready to cook, turn the Traeger on and set the temperature to 450°F and let it preheat for a minimum of 5 minutes.
2. Meanwhile, prepare the spice mix and for this, take a small bowl, place all of its ingredients in it and stir until mixed.
3. Take a large bowl, place shrimps in it, sprinkle with prepared spice mix, drizzle with oil and toss until well coated.
4. When the grill has preheated, open the lid, place shrimps on the grill grate, shut the grill and smoke for 3 minutes per side until firm and thoroughly cooked.
5. When done, transfer shrimps to a dish and then serve.

Cod With Lemon Herb Butter

Servings: 4

Cooking Time: 15 Minutes

Ingredients:

- 4 tablespoons butter
- 1 clove garlic, minced
- 1 tablespoon tarragon, chopped
- 1 tablespoon lemon juice
- 1 teaspoon lemon zest
- Salt and pepper to taste
- 1 lb. cod fillet

Directions:

1. When ready to cook, turn the Traeger on and set the temperature to 450°F. Preheat for 15 minutes while the lid is closed.
2. In a bowl, mix the butter, garlic, tarragon, lemon juice and lemon zest, salt and pepper.
3. Place the fish in a baking pan.
4. Spread the butter mixture on top.
5. Bake the fish for 15 minutes.

Wood Pellet Grilled Salmon Sandwich

Servings: 4

Cooking Time: 15 Minutes

Ingredients:

- Salmon Sandwiches
- 4 salmon fillets
- 1 tbsp olive oil
- Fin and feather rub
- 1 tbsp salt
- 4 toasted bun
- Butter lettuce
- Dill Aioli
- 1/2 cup mayonnaise
- 1/2 tbsp lemon zest
- 2 tbsp lemon juice
- 1/4 tbsp salt
- 1/2 tbsp fresh dill, minced

Directions:

1. Mix all the dill aioli ingredients and place them in the fridge.
2. When ready to cook, turn the Traeger on and set the temperature to 450°F.
3. Brush the salmon fillets with oil, rub, and salt. Place the fillets on the grill and cook until the internal temperature reaches 135°F.
4. Remove the fillets from the grill and let rest for 5 minutes.
5. Spread the aioli on the buns then top with salmon, lettuce, and the top bun.
6. Serve when hot.

Omega-3 Rich Salmon

👪 **Servings: 6**

🕐 **Cooking Time: 20 Minutes**

Ingredients:

- 6 (6-oz.) skinless salmon fillets
- 1/3 C. olive oil
- ¼ C. spice rub
- ¼ C. honey
- 2 tbsp. Sriracha
- 2 tbsp. fresh lime juice

Directions:

1. When ready to cook, turn the Traeger on and set the temperature to 300°F and preheat with closed lid for 15 minutes.
2. Coat salmon fillets with olive oil and season with rub evenly.
3. In a small bowl, mix together remaining ingredients.
4. Arrange salmon fillets onto the grill, flat-side up and cook for about 7-10 minutes per side, coating with honey mixture once halfway through.
5. Serve hot alongside remaining honey mixture.

Grilled Shrimp Scampi

👪 **Servings: 4**

🕐 **Cooking Time: 10 Minutes**

Ingredients:

- 1 lb raw shrimp, tail on
- 1/2 cup salted butter, melted
- 1/4 cup white wine, dry
- 1/2 tbsp fresh garlic, chopped
- 1 tbsp lemon juice
- 1/2 tbsp garlic powder
- 1/2 tbsp salt

Directions:

1. When ready to cook, turn the Traeger on and set the temperature to 400°F.
2. In a mixing bowl, mix butter, wine, garlic, and juice then pour in the cast iron. Let the mixture mix for 4 minutes.
3. Sprinkle garlic and salt on the shrimp then place it on the cast iron. Grill for 10 minutes with the lid closed.
4. Remove the shrimp from the grill and serve when hot. Enjoy.

Wood Pellet Grilled Lobster Tail

👪 **Servings: 2**

🕐 **Cooking Time: 15 Minutes**

Ingredients:

- 10 oz lobster tail
- 1/4 tbsp old bay seasoning
- 1/4 tbsp Himalayan sea salt
- 2 tbsp butter, melted
- 1 tbsp fresh parsley, chopped

Directions:

1. When ready to cook, turn the Traeger on and set the temperature to 450°F.
2. Slice the tails down the middle using a knife.
3. Season with seasoning and salt then place the tails on the grill grate.
4. Grill for 15 minutes or until the internal temperature reaches 140°F..
5. Remove the tails and drizzle with butter and garnish with parsley.
6. Serve and enjoy.

Togarashi Smoked Salmon

👪 **Servings: 10**

🕐 **Cooking Time: 20 Hours 15 Minutes**

Ingredients:

- Salmon filet - 2 large
- Togarashi for seasoning
- For Brine:
- Brown sugar - 1 cup
- Water - 4 cups
- Kosher salt - ⅓ cup

Directions:

1. Remove all the thorns from the fish filet.
2. Mix all the brine ingredients until the brown sugar is dissolved completely.
3. Put the mix in a big bowl and add the filet to it.
4. Leave the bowl to refrigerate for 16 hours.
5. After 16 hours, remove the salmon from this mix. Wash and dry it.
6. Place the salmon in the refrigerator for another 2-4 hours. (This step is important. DO NOT SKIP IT.)
7. Season your salmon filet with Togarashi.
8. When ready to cook, turn the Traeger on and set to Smoke and place the salmon on it.
9. Smoke for 4 hours.
10. Make sure the temperature does not go above 180°or below 130 degrees.
11. Remove from the grill and serve it warm with a side dish of your choice.

Wood Pellet Garlic Dill Smoked Salmon

👪 **Servings: 12**

🕐 **Cooking Time: 4 Hours**

Ingredients:

- 2 salmon fillets
- Brine
- 4 cups water
- 1 cup brown sugar
- 1/3 cup kosher salt
- Seasoning
- 3 tbsp minced garlic
- 1 tbsp fresh dill, chopped

Directions:

1. In a zip lock bag, combine the brine ingredients until all sugar has dissolved. Place the salmon in the bag and refrigerate overnight.
2. Remove the salmon from the brine, rinse with water and pat dry with a paper towel. Let it rest for 2-4 hours at room temperature.
3. Season the salmon with garlic and dill generously.
4. When ready to cook, turn the Traeger on and set the temperature to 130°F. Place the salmon on a cooling rack that is coated with cooking spray.
5. Place the rack in the smoker and close the lid.
6. Smoke the salmon for 4 hours until the smoke is between 130-180°F.
7. Remove the salmon from the grill and serve with crackers. Enjoy

Wood Pellet Smoked Buffalo Shrimp

👪 **Servings: 6**

🕐 **Cooking Time: 5 Minutes**

Ingredients:

- 1 lb raw shrimps peeled and deveined
- 1/2 tbsp salt
- 1/4 tbsp garlic salt
- 1/4 tbsp garlic powder
- 1/4 tbsp onion powder
- 1/2 cup buffalo sauce

Directions:

1. When ready to cook, turn the Traeger on and set the temperature to 450°F.
2. Coat the shrimp with both salts, garlic and onion powders.
3. Place the shrimp in a grill and cook for 3 minutes on each side.
4. Remove from the grill and toss in buffalo sauce. Serve with cheese, celery and napkins. Enjoy.

Wood Pellet Salt And Pepper Spot Prawn Skewers

👪 **Servings: 6**

🕐 **Cooking Time: 10 Minutes**

Ingredients:

- 2 lb spot prawns, clean
- 2 tbsp oil
- Salt and pepper to taste

Directions:

1. When ready to cook, turn the Traeger on and set the temperature to 400°F.
2. Meanwhile, soak the skewers then skewer with the prawns.
3. Brush with oil then season with salt and pepper to taste.
4. Place the skewers in the grill, close the lid, and cook for 5 minutes on each side.
5. Remove from the grill and serve. Enjoy.

Halibut

👪 **Servings: 4**

🕐 **Cooking Time: 3o Minutes**

Ingredients:

- 1-pound fresh halibut filet (cut into 4 equal sizes)
- 1 tbsp fresh lemon juice
- 2 garlic cloves (minced)
- 2 tsp soy sauce
- ½ tsp ground black pepper
- ½ tsp onion powder
- 2 tbsp honey
- ½ tsp oregano
- 1 tsp dried basil
- 2 tbsp butter (melted)
- Maple syrup for serving

Directions:

1. Combine the lemon juice, honey, soy sauce, onion powder, oregano, dried basil, pepper and garlic.
2. Brush the halibut filets generously with the filet the mixture. Wrap the filets with aluminum foil and refrigerate for 4 hours.
3. Remove the filets from the refrigerator and let them sit for about 2 hours, or until they are at room temperature.
4. When ready to cook, turn the Traeger on and set the temperature to 275°F.
5. The lid must not be opened for it to be preheated and reach 275°F 15 minutes, using fruit wood pellets.
6. Place the halibut filets directly on the grill grate and smoke for 30 minutes
7. Remove the filets from the grill and let them rest for 10 minutes.
8. Serve and top with maple syrup to taste

Wood-fired Halibut

👥 **Servings: 4**

🕐 **Cooking Time: 20 Minutes**

Ingredients:

- 1 pound halibut fillet
- 1 batch Dill Seafood Rub

Directions:

1. When ready to cook, turn the Traeger on and set the temperature to 325°F. Preheat the grill with the lid closed.
2. Sprinkle the halibut fillet on all sides with the rub. Using your hands, work the rub into the meat.
3. Place the halibut directly on the grill grate and grill until its internal temperature reaches 145°F. Remove the halibut from the grill and serve immediately.

Hot-smoked Salmon

👥 **Servings: 4**

🕐 **Cooking Time: 4 To 6 Hours**

Ingredients:

- 1 (2-pound) half salmon fillet
- 1 batch Dill Seafood Rub

Directions:

1. When ready to cook, turn the Traeger on and set the temperature to 180°F. Preheat the grill with the lid closed.
2. Season the salmon all over with the rub. Using your hands, work the rub into the flesh.
3. Place the salmon directly on the grill grate, skin-side down, and smoke until its internal temperature reaches 145°F. Remove the salmon from the grill and serve immediately.

Lobster Tails

👪 **Servings: 4**

🕐 **Cooking Time: 35 Minutes**

Ingredients:

- 2 lobster tails, each about 10 ounces
- For the Sauce:
- 2 tablespoons chopped parsley
- 1/4 teaspoon garlic salt
- 1 teaspoon paprika
- 1/4 teaspoon ground black pepper
- 1/4 teaspoon old bay seasoning
- 8 tablespoons butter, unsalted
- 2 tablespoons lemon juice

Directions:

1. When ready to cook, turn the Traeger on and set the temperature to 450°F and let it preheat for a minimum of 15 minutes.
2. Meanwhile, prepare the sauce and for this, take a small saucepan, place it over medium-low heat, add butter in it and when it melts, add remaining ingredients for the sauce and stir until combined, set aside until required.
3. Prepare the lobster and for this, cut the shell from the middle to the tail by using kitchen shears and then take the meat from the shell, keeping it attached at the base of the crab tail.
4. Then butterfly the crab meat by making a slit down the middle, then place lobster tails on a baking sheet and pour 1 tablespoon of sauce over each lobster tail, reserve the remaining sauce.
5. When the grill has preheated, open the lid, place crab tails on the grill grate, shut the grill and smoke for 30 minutes until opaque.
6. When done, transfer lobster tails to a dish and then serve with the remaining sauce.

Chilean Sea Bass

👪 **Servings: 6**

🕐 **Cooking Time: 40 Minutes**

Ingredients:

- 4 sea bass fillets, skinless, each about 6 ounces
- Chicken rub as needed
- 8 tablespoons butter, unsalted
- 2 tablespoons chopped thyme leaves
- Lemon slices for serving
- For the Marinade:
- 1 lemon, juiced
- 4 teaspoons minced garlic
- 1 tablespoon chopped thyme
- 1 teaspoon blackened rub
- 1 tablespoon chopped oregano
- 1/4 cup oil

Directions:

1. Prepare the marinade and for this, take a small bowl, place all of its ingredients in it, stir until well combined, and then pour the mixture into a large plastic bag.
2. Add fillets in the bag, seal it, turn it upside down to coat fillets with the marinade and let it marinate for a minimum of 30 minutes in the refrigerator.
3. When ready to cook, turn the Traeger on and set the temperature to 325°F and let it preheat for a minimum of 15 minutes.
4. Meanwhile, take a large baking pan and place butter on it.
5. When the grill has preheated, open the lid, place baking pan on the grill grate, and wait until butter melts.
6. Remove fillets from the marinade, pour marinade into the pan with melted butter, then season fillets with chicken rubs until coated on all sides, then place them into the pan, shut the grill and cook for 30 minutes until internal temperature reaches 160°F, frequently basting with the butter sauce.
7. When done, transfer fillets to a dish, sprinkle with thyme and then serve with lemon slices.

Grilled Salmon

👥 **Servings: 4**

🕐 **Cooking Time: 25 Minutes**

Ingredients:

- 1 (2-pound) half salmon fillet
- 3 tablespoons mayonnaise
- 1 batch Dill Seafood Rub

Directions:

1. When ready to cook, turn the Traeger on and set the temperature to 325°F. Preheat the grill with the lid closed.
2. Using your hands, rub the salmon fillet all over with the mayonnaise and sprinkle it with the rub.
3. Place the salmon directly on the grill grate, skin-side down, and grill until its internal temperature reaches 145°F. Remove the salmon from the grill and serve immediately.

Mango Shrimp

👥 **Servings: 4**

🕐 **Cooking Time: 15 Minutes**

Ingredients:

- 1lb. shrimp, peeled and deveined but tail intact
- 2tablespoons olive oil
- Mango seasoning

Directions:

1. When ready to cook, turn the Traeger on and set the temperature to 425°F.
2. Coat the shrimp with the oil and season with the mango seasoning.
3. Thread the shrimp into skewers.
4. Grill for 3 minutes per side.

Crazy Delicious Lobster Tails

👪 **Servings: 4**

🕐 **Cooking Time: 25 Minutes**

Ingredients:

* ½ C. butter, melted
* 2 garlic cloves, minced
* 2 tsp. fresh lemon juice
* Salt and freshly ground black pepper, to taste
* 4 (8-oz.) lobster tails

Directions:

1. When ready to cook, turn the Traeger on and set the temperature to 450°F and preheat with closed lid for 15 minutes.
2. In a metal pan, add all ingredients except for lobster tails and mix well.
3. Place the pan onto the grill and cook for about 10 minutes.
4. Meanwhile, cut down the top of the shell and expose lobster meat.
5. Remove pan of butter mixture from grill.
6. Coat the lobster meat with butter mixture.
7. Place the lobster tails onto the grill and cook for about 15 minutes, coating with butter mixture once halfway through.
8. Remove from grill and serve hot.

Cajun-blackened Shrimp

👪 **Servings: 4**

🕐 **Cooking Time: 20 Minutes**

Ingredients:

* 1 pound peeled and deveined shrimp, with tails on
* 1 batch Cajun Rub
* 8 tablespoons (1 stick) butter
* ¼ cup Worcestershire sauce

Directions:

1. When ready to cook, turn the Traeger on and set the temperature to 450°F. Preheat the grill with the lid closed and place a cast-iron skillet on the grill grate. Wait about 10 minutes after your grill has reached temperature, allowing the skillet to get hot.
2. Meanwhile, season the shrimp all over with the rub.
3. When the skillet is hot, place the butter in it to melt. Once the butter melts, stir in the Worcestershire sauce.
4. Add the shrimp and gently stir to coat. Smoke-braise the shrimp for about 10 minutes per side, until opaque and cooked through. Remove the shrimp from the grill and serve immediately.

Pacific Northwest Salmon

👪 **Servings: 4**

🕐 **Cooking Time: 1 Hours, 15 Minutes**

Ingredients:

- 1 (2-pound) half salmon fillet
- 1 batch Dill Seafood Rub
- 2 tablespoons butter, cut into 3 or 4 slices

Directions:

1. When ready to cook, turn the Traeger on and set the temperature to 180°F. Preheat the grill with the lid closed.
2. Season the salmon all over with the rub. Using your hands, work the rub into the flesh.
3. Place the salmon directly on the grill grate, skin-side down, and smoke for 1 hours.
4. Place the butter slices on the salmon, equally spaced. Increase the grill's temperature to 300°F and continue to cook until the salmon's internal temperature reaches 145°F. Remove the salmon from the grill and serve immediately.

Wood Pellet Teriyaki Smoked Shrimp

👪 **Servings: 6**

🕐 **Cooking Time: 10 Minutes**

Ingredients:

- 1 lb tail-on shrimp, uncooked
- 1/2 tbsp onion powder
- 1/2 tbsp salt
- 1/2 tbsp Garlic powder
- 4 tbsp Teriyaki sauce
- 4 tbsp sriracha mayo
- 2 tbsp green onion, minced

Directions:

1. Peel the shrimps leaving the tails then wash them removing any vein left over. Drain and pat with a paper towel to drain.
2. When ready to cook, turn the Traeger on and set the temperature to 450°F.
3. Season the shrimp with onion, salt, and garlic then place it on the grill to cook for 5 minutes on each side.
4. Remove the shrimp from the grill and toss it with teriyaki sauce. Serve garnished with mayo and onions. Enjoy.

Grilled Rainbow Trout

👥 Servings: 6

🕐 Cooking Time: 2 Hours

Ingredients:

- 6 rainbow trout, cleaned, butterfly
- For the Brine:
- 1/4 cup salt
- 1 tablespoon ground black pepper
- 1/2 cup brown sugar
- 2 tablespoons soy sauce
- 16 cups water

Directions:

1. Prepare the brine and for this, take a large container, add all of its ingredients in it, stir until sugar has dissolved, then add trout and let soak for 1 hours in the refrigerator.
2. When ready to cook, turn the Traeger on and set the temperature to 225°F and let it preheat for a minimum of 15 minutes.
3. Meanwhile, remove trout from the brine and pat dry with paper towels.
4. When the grill has preheated, open the lid, place trout on the grill grate, shut the grill and smoke for 2 hours until thoroughly cooked and tender.
5. When done, transfer trout to a dish and then serve.

Citrus Salmon

👥 Servings: 6

🕐 Cooking Time: 30 Minutes

Ingredients:

- 2 (1-lb.) salmon fillets
- Salt and freshly ground black pepper, to taste
- 1 tbsp. seafood seasoning
- 2 lemons, sliced
- 2 limes, sliced

Directions:

1. When ready to cook, turn the Traeger on and set the temperature to 225°F and preheat with closed lid for 15 minutes.
2. Season the salmon fillets with salt, black pepper and seafood seasoning evenly.
3. Place the salmon fillets onto the grill and top each with lemon and lime slices evenly.
4. Cook for about 30 minutes.
5. Remove the salmon fillets from grill and serve hot.

Barbeque Shrimp

👥 **Servings: 6**

🕐 **Cooking Time: 8 Minutes**

Ingredients:

- 2-pound raw shrimp (peeled and deveined)
- ¼ cup extra virgin olive oil
- ½ tsp paprika
- ½ tsp red pepper flakes
- 2 garlic cloves (minced)
- 1 tsp cumin
- 1 lemon (juiced)
- 1 tsp kosher salt
- 1 tbsp chili paste
- Bamboo or wooden skewers (soaked for 30 minutes, at least)

Directions:

1. Combine the pepper flakes, cumin, lemon, salt, chili, paprika, garlic and olive oil. Add the shrimp and toss to combine.
2. Transfer the shrimp and marinade into a zip-lock bag and refrigerate for 4 hours.
3. Let shrimp rest in room temperature after pulling it out from marinade
4. When ready to cook, turn the Traeger on and set to smoke, leaving the lid opened for 5 minutes, using hickory wood pellet.
5. Keep lid unopened and preheat the grill to "high" for 15 minutes.
6. Thread shrimps onto skewers and arrange the skewers on the grill grate.
7. Smoke shrimps for 8 minutes, 4 minutes per side.
8. Serve and enjoy.

Wood Pellet Rockfish

👥 **Servings: 6**

🕐 **Cooking Time: 20 Minutes**

Ingredients:

- 6 rockfish fillets
- 1 lemon, sliced
- 3/4 tbsp Himalayan salt
- 2 tbsp fresh dill, chopped
- 1/2 tbsp garlic powder
- 1/2 tbsp onion powder
- 6 tbsp butter

Directions:

1. When ready to cook, turn the Traeger on and set the temperature to 375°F.
2. Place the rockfish in a baking dish and season with salt, dill, garlic, and onion.
3. Place butter on top of the fish then close the lid. Cook for 20 minutes or until the fish is no longer translucent.
4. Remove from grill and let sit for 5 minutes before serving. enjoy.

Buttered Crab Legs

Servings: 4

Cooking Time: 10 Minutes

Ingredients:

- 12 tablespoons butter
- 1 tablespoon parsley, chopped
- 1 tablespoon tarragon, chopped
- 1 tablespoon chives, chopped
- 1 tablespoon lemon juice
- 4 lb. king crab legs, split in the center

Directions:

1. When ready to cook, turn the Traeger on and set the temperature to 375°F.
2. Preheat it for 15 minutes while lid is closed.
3. In a pan over medium heat, simmer the butter, herbs and lemon juice for 2 minutes.
4. Place the crab legs on the grill.
5. Pour half of the sauce on top.
6. Grill for 10 minutes.
7. Serve with the reserved butter sauce.

Grilled Blackened Salmon

Servings: 4

Cooking Time: 30 Minutes

Ingredients:

- 4 salmon fillet
- Blackened dry rub
- Italian seasoning powder

Directions:

1. Season salmon fillets with dry rub and seasoning powder.
2. When ready to cook, turn the Traeger on and set the temperature to 325°F.
3. Grill in the Traeger at 325°F for 10 to 15 minutes per side.

5

Vegetable & Vegetarian Recipes

Whole Roasted Cauliflower With Garlic Parmesan Butter

👥 **Servings: 5**

🕐 **Cooking Time: 45 Minutes**

Ingredients:

- 1/4 cup olive oil
- Salt and pepper to taste
- 1 cauliflower, fresh
- 1/2 cup butter, melted
- 1/4 cup parmesan cheese, grated
- 2 garlic cloves, minced
- 1/2 tbsp parsley, chopped

Directions:

1. When ready to cook, turn the Traeger on.
2. Preheat with the lid closed for 15 minutes.
3. Meanwhile, brush the cauliflower with oil then season with salt and pepper.
4. Place the cauliflower in a cast iron and place it on a grill grate.
5. Cook for 45 minutes or until the cauliflower is golden brown and tender.
6. Meanwhile, mix butter, cheese, garlic, and parsley in a mixing bowl.
7. In the last 20 minutes of cooking, add the butter mixture.
8. Remove the cauliflower from the grill and top with more cheese and parsley if you desire. Enjoy.

Grilled Baby Carrots And Fennel With Romesco

👥 **Servings: 8 To 12**

🕐 **Cooking Time: 45 Minutes**

Ingredients:

- 1 Pound Slender Rainbow Carrots
- 2 Whole Fennel, bulb
- 2 Tablespoon extra-virgin olive oil
- 1 Teaspoon salt
- 2 Tablespoon extra-virgin olive oil
- To Taste salt
- 1 Tablespoon fresh thyme

Directions:

1. When ready to cook, turn the Traeger on and set the temperature to High and preheat with lid closed for 15 minutes. For optimal results, set to 500☐ if available.
2. Trim the carrot tops to 1". Peel the carrots and halve any larger ones so they are all about 1/2" thick. Cut the fennel bulbs lengthwise into 1/2" thick slices.
3. Place the fennel and potato slices in a large mixing bowl. Drizzle with 2 Tbsp of the olive oil and a teaspoon of salt.
4. Toss to coat the vegetables evenly with the oil.
5. Place the carrots on a sheet pan. Drizzle with the additional 2 Tbsp of olive oil and a generous pinch of salt. Brush the olive oil over the carrots to distribute evenly.
6. Add the potatoes and fennel slices to the sheet pan. Nestle a few sprigs of herbs into the vegetables as well.
7. Place the pan directly on the grill grate and cook, stirring occasionally until the vegetables are browned and softened, about 35-45 minutes.
8. Allow to cool and serve with the Smoked Romesco Sauce. Enjoy!

Grilled Cherry Tomato Skewers

👪 **Servings: 4**

🕐 **Cooking Time: 50 Minutes**

Ingredients:

- 24 cherry tomatoes
- 1/4 cup olive oil
- 3tbsp balsamic vinegar
- 4garlic cloves, minced
- 1tbsp fresh thyme, finely chopped
- 1tsp kosher salt
- 1tsp ground black pepper
- 2tbsp chives, finely chopped

Directions:

1. When ready to cook, turn the Traeger on and set the temperature to 425°F.
2. In a medium-sized bowl, mix olive oil, balsamic vinegar, garlic, and thyme. Add tomatoes and toss to coat.
3. Let tomatoes sit in the marinade at room temperature for about 30 minutes.
4. Remove tomatoes from marinade and thread 4 tomatoes per skewer.
5. Season both sides of each skewer with kosher salt and ground pepper.
6. Place on grill grate and grill for about 3 minutes on each side, or until each side is slightly charred.
7. Remove from grill and allow to rest for about 5 minutes. Garnish with chives, then serve and enjoy!

Crispy Maple Bacon Brussels Sprouts

👪 **Servings: 6**

🕐 **Cooking Time: 1 Hours**

Ingredients:

- 1lb brussels sprouts, trimmed and quartered
- 6 slices thick-cut bacon
- 3tbsp maple syrup
- 1tsp olive oil
- 1/2 tsp kosher salt
- 1/2 tsp ground black pepper

Directions:

1. When ready to cook, turn the Traeger on and set the temperature to 425°F.
2. Cut bacon into 1/2 inch thick slices.
3. Place brussels sprouts in a single layer in the cast iron skillet. Drizzle with olive oil and maple syrup, then toss to coat. Sprinkle bacon slices on top then season with kosher salt and black pepper.
4. Place skillet in the pellet grill and roast for about 40 to 45 minutes, or until the brussels sprouts are caramelized and brown.
5. Remove skillet from grill and allow brussels sprouts to cool for about 5 to 10 minutes. Serve and enjoy!

Smoked Healthy Cabbage

Servings: 5

Cooking Time: 2 Hours

Ingredients:

- 1head cabbage, cored
- 4tablespoons butter
- 2tablespoons rendered bacon fat
- 1chicken bouillon cube
- 1teaspoon fresh ground black pepper
- 1garlic clove, minced

Directions:

1. When ready to cook, turn the Traeger on and set the temperature to 240°F, using your preferred wood.
2. Fill the hole of your cored cabbage with butter, bouillon cube, bacon fat, pepper and garlic
3. Wrap the cabbage in foil about two-thirds of the way up
4. Make sure to leave the top open
5. Transfer to your smoker rack and smoke for 2 hours
6. Unwrap and enjoy!

Grilled Ratatouille Salad

Servings: 6

Cooking Time: 25 Minutes

Ingredients:

- 1 Whole sweet potatoes
- 1 Whole red onion, diced
- 1 Whole zucchini
- 1 Whole Squash
- 1 Large Tomato, diced
- As Needed vegetable oil
- As Needed salt and pepper

Directions:

1. When ready to cook, turn the Traeger on. Preheat grill to high setting with the lid closed for 10-15 minutes.
2. Slice all vegetables to a ¼ inch thickness.
3. Lightly brush each vegetable with oil and season with Traeger's Veggie Shake or salt and pepper.
4. Place sweet potato, onion, zucchini, and squash on grill grate and grill for 20 minutes or until tender, turn halfway through.
5. Add tomato slices to the grill during the last 5 minutes of cooking time.
6. For presentation, alternate vegetables while layering them vertically. Enjoy!

Roasted Vegetable Medley

Servings: 4 To 6

Cooking Time: 50 Minutes

Ingredients:

- 2medium potatoes, cut to 1 inch wedges
- 2red bell peppers, cut into 1 inch cubes
- 1small butternut squash, peeled and cubed to 1 inch cube
- 1red onion, cut to 1 inch cubes
- 1cup broccoli, trimmed
- 2tbsp olive oil
- 1tbsp balsamic vinegar
- 1tbsp fresh rosemary, minced
- 1tbsp fresh thyme, minced
- 1tsp kosher salt
- 1tsp ground black pepper

Directions:

1. When ready to cook, turn the Traeger on and set the temperature to 425°F.
2. In a large bowl, combine potatoes, peppers, squash, and onion.
3. In a small bowl, whisk together olive oil, balsamic vinegar, rosemary, thyme, salt, and pepper.
4. Pour marinade over vegetables and toss to coat. Allow resting for about 15 minutes.
5. Place marinated vegetables into a grill basket, and place a grill basket on the grill grate. Cook for about 30-40 minutes, occasionally tossing in the grill basket.
6. Remove veggies from grill and transfer to a serving dish. Allow to cool for 5 minutes, then serve and enjoy!

Smoked Deviled Eggs

Servings: 4 To 6

Cooking Time: 50 Minutes

Ingredients:

- 6 large eggs
- 1slice bacon
- 1/4 cup mayonnaise
- 1tsp Dijon mustard
- 1tsp apple cider vinegar
- 1/4 tsp paprika
- Pinch of kosher salt
- 1tbsp chives, chopped

Directions:

1. When ready to cook, turn the Traeger on and set the temperature to 180°F and turn smoke setting on, if applicable.
2. Bring a pot of water to a boil. Add eggs and hard boil eggs for about 12 minutes.
3. Remove eggs from pot and place them into an ice-water bath. Once eggs have cooled completely, peel them and slice in half lengthwise.
4. Place sliced eggs on grill, yolk side up. Smoke for 30 to 45 minutes, depending on how much smoky flavor you want.
5. While eggs smoke, cook bacon until it's crispy.
6. Remove eggs from the grill and allow to cool on a plate.
7. Remove the yolks and place all of them in a small bowl. Place the egg whites on a plate.
8. Mash yolks with a fork and add mayonnaise, mustard, apple cider vinegar, paprika, and salt. Stir until combined.
9. Spoon a scoop of yolk mixture back into each egg white.
10. Sprinkle paprika, chives, and crispy bacon bits to garnish. Serve and enjoy!

Wood Pellet Smoked Acorn Squash

👪 Servings: 6

🕐 Cooking Time: 2 Hours

Ingredients:

- 3 tbsp olive oil
- 3 acorn squash, halved and seeded
- 1/4 cup unsalted butter
- 1/4 cup brown sugar
- 1 tbsp cinnamon, ground
- 1 tbsp chili powder
- 1 tbsp nutmeg, ground

Directions:

1. Brush olive oil on the acorn squash cut sides then cover the halves with foil. Poke holes on the foil to allow steam and smoke through.
2. When ready to cook, turn the Traeger on and set the temperature to 225°F and smoke the squash for 1-1/2-2 hours.
3. Remove the squash from the smoker and allow it to sit.
4. Meanwhile, melt butter, sugar and spices in a saucepan. Stir well to combine.
5. Remove the foil from the squash and spoon the butter mixture in each squash half. Enjoy.

Grilled Carrots And Asparagus

👪 Servings: 6

🕐 Cooking Time: 30 Minutes

Ingredients:

- 1 pound whole carrots, with tops
- 1 bunch of asparagus, ends trimmed
- Sea salt as needed
- 1 teaspoon lemon zest
- 2 tablespoons honey
- 2 tablespoons olive oil

Directions:

1. When ready to cook, turn the Traeger on and set the temperature to 450°F and let it preheat for a minimum of 15 minutes.
2. Meanwhile, take a medium dish, place asparagus in it, season with sea salt, drizzle with oil and toss until mixed.
3. Take a medium bowl, place carrots in it, drizzle with honey, sprinkle with sea salt and toss until combined.
4. When the grill has preheated, open the lid, place asparagus and carrots on the grill grate, shut the grill and smoke for 30 minutes.
5. When done, transfer vegetables to a dish, sprinkle with lemon zest, and then serve.

Georgia Sweet Onion Bake

Servings: 6

Cooking Time: 1 Hours

Ingredients:

- Nonstick cooking spray or butter, for greasing
- 4 large Vidalia or other sweet onions
- 8 tablespoons (1 stick) unsalted butter, melted
- 4 chicken bouillon cubes
- 1 cup grated Parmesan cheese

Directions:

1. When ready to cook, turn the Traeger on and set the temperature to 350°F. Preheat with the lid closed.
2. Coat a high-sided baking pan with cooking spray or butter.
3. Peel the onions and cut into quarters, separating into individual petals.
4. Spread the onions out in the prepared pan and pour the melted butter over them.
5. Crush the bouillon cubes and sprinkle over the buttery onion pieces, then top with the cheese.
6. Transfer the pan to the grill, close the lid, and smoke for 30 minutes.
7. Remove the pan from the grill, cover tightly with aluminum foil, and poke several holes all over to vent.
8. Place the pan back on the grill, close the lid, and smoke for an additional 30 to 45 minutes.
9. Uncover the onions, stir, and serve hot.

Grilled Corn With Honey & Butter

Servings: 4

Cooking Time: 10 Minutes

Ingredients:

- 6 pieces corn
- 2 tablespoons olive oil
- 1/2 cup butter
- 1/2 cup honey
- 1 tablespoon smoked salt
- Pepper to taste

Directions:

1. When ready to cook, turn the Traeger on and set the temperature to High. Preheat the Traeger for 15 minutes while the lid is closed.
2. Brush the corn with oil and butter.
3. Grill the corn for 10 minutes, turning from time to time.
4. Mix honey and butter.
5. Brush corn with this mixture and sprinkle with smoked salt and pepper.

Wood Pellet Bacon Wrapped Jalapeno Poppers

 Servings: 6

 Cooking Time: 20 Minutes

Ingredients:

- 6 jalapenos, fresh
- 4 oz cream cheese
- 1/2 cup cheddar cheese, shredded
- 1 tbsp vegetable rub
- 12 slices cut bacon

Directions:

1. When ready to cook, turn the Traeger on and set the temperature to 375°F.
2. Slice the jalapenos lengthwise and scrape the seed and membrane. Rinse them with water and set aside.
3. In a mixing bowl, mix cream cheese, cheddar cheese, vegetable rub until well mixed.
4. Fill the jalapeno halves with the mixture then wrap with the bacon pieces.
5. Smoke for 20 minutes or until the bacon crispy.
6. Serve and enjoy.

Wood Pellet Grilled Zucchini Squash Spears

Servings: 5

Cooking Time: 10 Minutes

Ingredients:

- 4 zucchini, cleaned and ends cut
- 2 tbsp olive oil
- 1 tbsp sherry vinegar
- 2 thyme, leaves pulled
- Salt and pepper to taste

Directions:

1. Cut the zucchini into halves then cut each half thirds.
2. Add the rest of the ingredients in a ziplock bag with the zucchini pieces. Toss to mix well.
3. When ready to cook, turn the Traeger on and set the temperature to 350°F. Preheat with the lid closed for 15 minutes.
4. Remove the zucchini from the bag and place them on the grill grate with the cut side down.
5. Cook for 4 minutes per side or until the zucchini are tender.
6. Remove from grill and serve with thyme leaves. Enjoy.

Easy Smoked Vegetables

Servings: 6

Cooking Time: 1 ½ Hours

Ingredients:

- 1 cup of pecan wood chips
- 1 ear fresh corn, silk strands removed, and husks, cut corn into 1-inch pieces
- 1 medium yellow squash, 1/2-inch slices
- 1 small red onion, thin wedges
- 1 small green bell pepper, 1-inch strips
- 1 small red bell pepper, 1-inch strips
- 1 small yellow bell pepper, 1-inch strips
- 1 cup mushrooms, halved
- 2 tbsp vegetable oil
- Vegetable seasonings

Directions:

1. Take a large bowl and toss all the vegetables together in it. Sprinkle it with seasoning and coat all the vegetables well with it.
2. Place the wood chips and a bowl of water in the smoker.
3. Preheat the smoker at 100°F or ten minutes.
4. Put the vegetables in a pan and add to the middle rack of the electric smoker.
5. Smoke for thirty minutes until the vegetable becomes tender.
6. When done, serve, and enjoy.

Wood Pellet Grilled Mexican Street Corn

Servings: 6

Cooking Time: 25 Minutes

Ingredients:

- 6 ears of corn on the cob, shucked
- 1 tbsp olive oil
- Kosher salt and pepper to taste
- 1/4 cup mayo
- 1/4cup sour cream
- 1 tbsp garlic paste
- 1/2 tbsp chili powder
- Pinch of ground red pepper
- 1/2 cup cotija cheese, crumbled
- 1/4 cup cilantro, chopped
- 6 lime wedges

Directions:

1. Brush the corn with oil and sprinkle with salt.
2. When ready to cook, turn the Traeger on and set the temperature to 350°F. Place the corn it and cook for 25 minutes as you turn it occasionally.
3. Meanwhile mix mayo, cream, garlic, chili, and red pepper until well combined.
4. When the corn is cooked remove from the grill, let it rest for some minutes then brush with the mayo mixture.
5. Sprinkle cotija cheese, more chili powder, and cilantro. Serve with lime wedges. Enjoy.

Grilled Potato Salad

Servings: 8

Cooking Time: 10 Minutes

Ingredients:

- 1 ½ pound fingerling potatoes, halved lengthwise
- 1 small jalapeno, sliced
- 10 scallions
- 2 teaspoons salt
- 2 tablespoons rice vinegar
- 2 teaspoons lemon juice
- 2/3 cup olive oil, divided

Directions:

1. When ready to cook, turn the Traeger on and set the temperature to 450°F and let it preheat for a minimum of 5 minutes.
2. Meanwhile, prepare scallions, and for this, brush them with some oil.
3. When the grill has preheated, open the lid, place scallions on the grill grate, shut the grill and smoke for 3 minutes until lightly charred.
4. Then transfer scallions to a cutting board, let them cool for 5 minutes, then cut into slices and set aside until required.
5. Brush potatoes with some oil, season with some salt and black pepper, place potatoes on the grill grate, shut the grill and smoke for 5 minutes until thoroughly cooked.
6. Then take a large bowl, pour in remaining oil, add salt, lemon juice, and vinegar and stir until combined.
7. Add grilled scallion and potatoes, toss until well mixed, taste to adjust seasoning and then serve.

Smoked Tofu

Servings: 4

Cooking Time: 41 Hours And 30 Minutes

Ingredients:

- 400g plain tofu
- Sesame oil

Directions:

1. When ready to cook, turn the Traeger on and set the temperature to 225°F. Preheat while adding wood chips and water to it.
2. Till that time, take the tofu out of the packet and let it rest
3. Slice the tofu in one-inch thick pieces and apply sesame oil
4. Place the tofu inside the smoker for 45 minutes while adding water and wood chips after one hours.
5. Once cooked, take them out and serve!

Garlic And Herb Smoke Potato

👥 **Servings: 6**

🕐 **Cooking Time: 2 Hours**

Ingredients:

- 1.5 pounds bag of Gemstone Potatoes
- 1/4 cup Parmesan, fresh grated
- For the Marinade
- 2 tbsp olive oil
- 6 garlic cloves, freshly chopped
- 1/2 tsp dried oregano
- 1/2 tsp dried basil
- 1/2 tsp dried dill
- 1/2 tsp salt
- 1/2 tsp dried Italian seasoning
- 1/4 tsp ground pepper

Directions:

1. When ready to cook, turn the Traeger on and set the temperature to 225°F.
2. Wash the potatoes thoroughly and add them to a sealable plastic bag.
3. Add garlic cloves, basil, salt, Italian seasoning, dill, oregano, and olive oil to the zip lock bag. Shake.
4. Place in the fridge for 2 hours to marinate.
5. Next, take an Aluminum foil and put 2 tbsp of water along with the coated potatoes. Fold the foil so that the potatoes are sealed in
6. Place in the preheated smoker.
7. Smoke for 2 hours
8. Remove the foil and pour the potatoes into a bowl.
9. Serve with grated Parmesan cheese.

Roasted Parmesan Cheese Broccoli

👥 **Servings: 3 To 4**

🕐 **Cooking Time: 45 Minutes**

Ingredients:

- 3cups broccoli, stems trimmed
- 1tbsp lemon juice
- 1tbsp olive oil
- 2garlic cloves, minced
- 1/2 tsp kosher salt
- 1/2 tsp ground black pepper
- 1tsp lemon zest
- 1/8 cup parmesan cheese, grated

Directions:

1. When ready to cook, turn the Traeger on and set the temperature to 375°F.
2. Place broccoli in a resealable bag. Add lemon juice, olive oil, garlic cloves, salt, and pepper. Seal the bag and toss to combine. Let the mixture marinate for 30 minutes.
3. Pour broccoli into a grill basket. Place basket on grill grates to roast. Grill broccoli for 14-18 minutes, flipping broccoli halfway through. Grill until tender yet a little crispy on the outside.
4. Remove broccoli from grill and place on a serving dish—zest with lemon and top with grated parmesan cheese. Serve immediately and enjoy!

Roasted Spicy Tomatoes

Servings: 4

Cooking Time: 1 Hours And 30 Minutes

Ingredients:

- 2 lb. large tomatoes, sliced in half
- Olive oil
- 2 tablespoons garlic, chopped
- 3 tablespoons parsley, chopped
- Salt and pepper to taste
- Hot pepper sauce

Directions:

1. When ready to cook, turn the Traeger on and set the temperature to 400°F.
2. Preheat it for 15 minutes while the lid is closed.
3. Add tomatoes to a baking pan.
4. Drizzle with oil and sprinkle with garlic, parsley, salt and pepper.
5. Roast for 1 hours and 30 minutes.
6. Drizzle with hot pepper sauce and serve.

Blt Pasta Salad

Servings: 6

Cooking Time: 35 To 45 Minutes

Ingredients:

- 1 pound thick-cut bacon
- 16 ounces bowtie pasta, cooked according to package directions and drained
- 2 tomatoes, chopped
- ½ cup chopped scallions
- ½ cup Italian dressing
- ½ cup ranch dressing
- 1 tablespoon chopped fresh basil
- 1 teaspoon salt
- 1 teaspoon freshly ground black pepper
- 1 teaspoon garlic powder
- 1 head lettuce, cored and torn

Directions:

1. When ready to cook, turn the Traeger on and set the temperature to 225°F. Preheat with the lid closed.
2. Arrange the bacon slices on the grill grate, close the lid, and cook for 30 to 45 minutes, flipping after 20 minutes, until crisp.
3. Remove the bacon from the grill and chop.
4. In a large bowl, combine the chopped bacon with the cooked pasta, tomatoes, scallions, Italian dressing, ranch dressing, basil, salt, pepper, and garlic powder. Refrigerate until ready to serve.
5. Toss in the lettuce just before serving to keep it from wilting.

Wood Pellet Grill Spicy Sweet Potatoes

Servings: 6

Cooking Time: 35 Minutes

Ingredients:

- 2 lb sweet potatoes, cut into chunks
- 1 red onion, chopped
- 2 tbsp oil
- 2 tbsp orange juice
- 1 tbsp roasted cinnamon
- 1 tbsp salt
- 1/4 tbsp Chiptole chili pepper

Directions:

1. When ready to cook, turn the Traeger on and set the temperature to 425°F. Preheat with the lid closed.
2. Toss the sweet potatoes with onion, oil, and juice.
3. In a mixing bowl, mix cinnamon, salt, and pepper then sprinkle the mixture over the sweet potatoes.
4. Spread the potatoes on a lined baking dish in a single layer.
5. Place the baking dish in the grill and grill for 30 minutes or until the sweet potatoes ate tender.
6. Serve and enjoy.

Wood Pellet Grilled Asparagus And Honey Glazed Carrots

Servings: 5

Cooking Time: 35 Minutes

Ingredients:

- 1 bunch asparagus, trimmed ends
- 1 lb carrots, peeled
- 2 tbsp olive oil
- Sea salt to taste
- 2 tbsp honey
- Lemon zest

Directions:

1. Sprinkle the asparagus with oil and sea salt. Drizzle the carrots with honey and salt.
2. When ready to cook, turn the Traeger on and set the temperature to 165°F. Preheat with the lid closed for 15 minutes.
3. Place the carrots in the wood pellet and cook for 15 minutes. Add asparagus and cook for 20 more minutes or until cooked through.
4. Top the carrots and asparagus with lemon zest. Enjoy.

Potato Fries With Chipotle Peppers

Servings: 4

Cooking Time: 30 Minutes

Ingredients:

- 4 potatoes, sliced into strips
- 3 tablespoons olive oil
- Salt and pepper to taste
- 1 cup mayonnaise
- 2 chipotle peppers in adobo sauce
- 2 tablespoons lime juice

Directions:

1. When ready to cook, turn the Traeger on and set the temperature to high.
2. Preheat it for 15 minutes while the lid is closed.
3. Coat the potato strips with oil.
4. Sprinkle with salt and pepper.
5. Put a baking pan on the grate.
6. Transfer potato strips to the pan.
7. Cook potatoes until crispy.
8. Mix the remaining ingredients.
9. Pulse in a food processor until pureed.
10. Serve potato fries with chipotle dip.

Sweet Potato Fries

Servings: 4

Cooking Time: 40 Minutes

Ingredients:

- 3 sweet potatoes, sliced into strips
- 4 tablespoons olive oil
- 2 tablespoons fresh rosemary, chopped
- Salt and pepper to taste

Directions:

1. When ready to cook, turn the Traeger on and set the temperature to 450°F.
2. Preheat it for 10 minutes.
3. Spread the sweet potato strips in the baking pan.
4. Toss in olive oil and sprinkle with rosemary, salt and pepper.
5. Cook for 15 minutes.
6. Flip and cook for another 15 minutes.
7. Flip and cook for 10 more minutes.

Feisty Roasted Cauliflower

👪 **Servings: 4**

🕐 **Cooking Time: 10 Minutes**

Ingredients:

- 1cauliflower head, cut into florets
- 1tablespoon oil
- 1cup parmesan, grated
- 2garlic cloves, crushed
- ½ teaspoon pepper
- ½ teaspoon salt
- ¼ teaspoon paprika

Directions:

1. When ready to cook, turn the Traeger on and set the temperature to 180°F.
2. Transfer florets to smoker and smoke for 1 hours.
3. Take a bowl and add all ingredients except cheese.
4. Once smoking is done, remove florets.
5. Increase temperature to 450°F, brush florets with the brush and transfer to grill.
6. Smoke for 10 minutes more.
7. Sprinkle cheese on top and let them sit (Lid closed) until cheese melts.
8. Serve and enjoy!

Sweet Jalapeño Cornbread

👪 **Servings: 12**

🕐 **Cooking Time: 50 Minutes**

Ingredients:

- 2/3 cup margarine, softened
- 2/3 cup white sugar
- 2cups cornmeal
- 1.1/3 cups all-purpose flour
- 4tsp baking powder
- 1tsp kosher salt
- 3eggs
- 1.2/3 cups milk
- 1cup jalapeños, deseeded and chopped
- Butter, to line baking dish

Directions:

1. When ready to cook, turn the Traeger on and set the temperature to 400°F.
2. Beat margarine and sugar together in a medium-sized bowl until smooth.
3. In another bowl, combine cornmeal, flour, baking powder, and salt.
4. In a third bowl, combine and whisk eggs and milk.
5. Pour 1/3 of the milk mixture and 1/3 of the flour mixture into the margarine mixture at a time, whisking just until mixed after each pour.
6. Once thoroughly combined, stir in chopped jalapeño.
7. Lightly butter the bottom of the baking dish. Pour cornbread mixture evenly into the baking dish.
8. Place dish on grill grates and close the lid. Cook for about 23-25 minutes, or until thoroughly cooked. The way to test is by inserting a toothpick into the center of the cornbread - it should come out clean once removed.
9. Remove dish from the grill and allow to rest for 10 minutes before slicing and serving.

Wood Pellet Grilled Vegetables

👪 **Servings: 8**

🕐 **Cooking Time: 15 Minutes**

Ingredients:

- 1 veggie tray
- 1/4 cup vegetable oil
- 2 tbsp veggie seasoning

Directions:

1. When ready to cook, turn the Traeger on and set the temperature to 375°F.
2. Toss the vegetables in oil then place on a sheet pan.
3. Sprinkle with veggie seasoning then place on the hot grill.
4. Grill for 15 minutes or until the veggies are cooked.
5. Let rest then serve. Enjoy.

Roasted Veggies & Hummus

👪 **Servings: 4**

🕐 **Cooking Time: 20 Minutes**

Ingredients:

- 1 white onion, sliced into wedges
- 2 cups butternut squash
- 2 cups cauliflower, sliced into florets
- 1 cup mushroom buttons
- Olive oil
- Salt and pepper to taste
- Hummus

Directions:

1. When ready to cook, turn the Traeger on and set the temperature to high.
2. Preheat it for 10 minutes while the lid is closed.
3. Add the veggies to a baking pan.
4. Roast for 20 minutes.
5. Serve roasted veggies with hummus.

Roasted Okra

Servings: 4

Cooking Time: 30 Minutes

Ingredients:

- Nonstick cooking spray or butter, for greasing
- 1 pound whole okra
- 2 tablespoons extra-virgin olive oil
- 2 teaspoons seasoned salt
- 2 teaspoons freshly ground black pepper

Directions:

1. When ready to cook, turn the Traeger on and set the temperature to 400°F. Preheat with the lid closed. Alternatively, preheat your oven to 400°F.
2. Line a shallow rimmed baking pan with aluminum foil and coat with cooking spray.
3. Arrange the okra on the pan in a single layer. Drizzle with the olive oil, turning to coat. Season on all sides with the salt and pepper.
4. Place the baking pan on the grill grate, close the lid, and smoke for 30 minutes, or until crisp and slightly charred. Alternatively, roast in the oven for 30 minutes.
5. Serve hot.

Roasted Root Vegetables

Servings: 6

Cooking Time: 45 Minutes

Ingredients:

- 1 large red onion, peeled
- 1 bunch of red beets, trimmed, peeled
- 1 large yam, peeled
- 1 bunch of golden beets, trimmed, peeled
- 1 large parsnips, peeled
- 1 butternut squash, peeled
- 1 large carrot, peeled
- 6 garlic cloves, peeled
- 3 tablespoons thyme leaves
- Salt as needed
- 1 cinnamon stick
- Ground black pepper as needed
- 3 tablespoons olive oil
- 2 tablespoons honey

Directions:

1. When ready to cook, turn the Traeger on and set the temperature to 450°F and let it preheat for a minimum of 15 minutes.
2. Meanwhile, cut all the vegetables into ½-inch pieces, place them in a large bowl, add garlic, thyme, and cinnamon, drizzle with oil and toss until mixed.
3. Take a large cookie sheet, line it with foil, spread with vegetables, and then season with salt and black pepper.
4. When the grill has preheated, open the lid, place prepared cookie sheet on the grill grate, shut the grill and smoke for 45 minutes until tender.
5. When done, transfer vegetables to a dish, drizzle with honey, and then serve.

6
Other Favorite Recipes

Grilled Venison Kebab

👪 **Servings: 4**

🕐 **Cooking Time: 15 Minutes**

Ingredients:

- 1 venison, sliced into cubes
- 2 red onions, sliced into wedges
- 2 red bell pepper, sliced into 2
- 2 yellow bell pepper, sliced into 2
- Olive oil
- Salt and pepper to taste
- 2 tablespoons lemon juice
- 1 1/2 tablespoons fresh mint leaves, chopped
- 1 1/2 tablespoons parsley, chopped

Directions:

1. Add the venison chunks, onion and bell peppers in a bowl.
2. Coat with olive oil and season with salt and pepper.
3. Thread onto skewers alternately.
4. In another bowl, mix lemon juice, mint leaves and parsley. Set aside.
5. When ready to cook, turn the Traeger on and set the temperature to high. Preheat while the lid is closed for 10 minutes.
6. Grill the kebabs for 7 to 8 minutes per side.
7. Brush with the lemon mixture in the last minute of cooking.

Grilled Chili Burger

👪 **Servings: 8**

🕐 **Cooking Time: 20 Minutes**

Ingredients:

- 1 tsp of chili powder
- 4 tsp of butter
- 2 pounds of round steak, twice-grounded
- 1 clove of garlic
- Salt and ground pepper, preferably freshly ground
- 1/4 cup of bread crumbs

Directions:

1. When ready to cook, turn the Traeger on and set the temperature to 300°F . Use maple pellets for a robust and woody taste.
2. Pour the meat inside a bowl and add the rest of the ingredients. Mix until well-combined. Mold the meat mixture to form 8 patties.
3. Arrange patties on the preheated cooking grid and grill for 10 minutes before flipping and grilling the other side for another 10 minutes.
4. Serve immediately with hamburger buns.

Smoked Teriyaki Tuna

👥 **Servings: 4**

🕐 **Cooking Time: 2 Hours**

Ingredients:

- Tuna steaks, 1 oz.
- 2 c. marinade, teriyaki
- Alder wood chips soaked in water

Directions:

1. Slice tuna into thick slices of 2 inch. Place your tuna slices and marinade then set in your fridge for about 3 hours
2. After 3 hours, remove the tuna from the marinade and pat dry. Let the tuna air dry in your fridge for 2-4 hours. When ready to cook, turn the Traeger on and set the temperature to 180°F.
3. Place the Tuna on a Teflon-coated fiberglass and place them directly on your grill grates. Smoke the Tuna for about an hours until the internal temperature reaches 145°F.
4. Remove the tuna from your grill and let them rest for 10 minutes. Serve!

Grilled Pepper Steak With Mushroom Sauce

👥 **Servings: 4**

🕐 **Cooking Time: 30 Minutes**

Ingredients:

- 2 cloves garlic, minced
- 1 tablespoon Worcestershire sauce
- 1/2 cup Dijon mustard
- 2 tablespoons bourbon
- 4 tenderloin steaks
- Salt and tri-color peppercorns to taste
- 1 tablespoon olive oil
- 1 onion, diced
- 1/2 cup white wine
- 1/2 cup chicken broth
- 16 oz. mushrooms, sliced
- ½ cup cream
- Salt and pepper to taste

Directions:

1. In a bowl, mix the garlic, Worcestershire sauce, Dijon mustard, and bourbon.
2. Spread the mixture on both sides of the steak and wrap with foil.
3. Marinate at room temperature for 1 hours.
4. Unwrap and season the steak with salt and peppercorns.
5. Press the peppercorns into the steak.
6. When ready to cook, turn the Traeger on and set the temperature to 180°F. Preheat your Traeger for 15 minutes while the lid is closed.
7. Grill the steaks for 30 minutes, flipping once or twice.
8. Make the mushroom gravy by cooking onion in olive oil in a pan over medium heat.
9. Add mushrooms.
10. Pour in the broth and white wine.
11. Simmer for 5 minutes.
12. Stir in the cream.
13. Season with salt and pepper.
14. Serve steaks with sauce.

Mutton Barbecued And Black Dip

👪 **Servings:7**

🕐 **Cooking Time: 7 Hours 20 Minutes**

Ingredients:

- Kosher or sea salt
- 7 hamburger buns
- 2 Tbsp of butter
- Sliced dill pickle
- 6 pounds of lamb shoulder
- Black dip

Directions:

1. Season lamb with salt and pepper
2. When ready to cook, turn the Traeger on and set the temperature to 250°F. Preheat the grill for 15 minutes at 250°F. Use pecan wood pellets.
3. Put the lamb inside black dip, then transfer it to the smoking rack. Smoke the lamb for 7 hours.
4. Put the already smoked lamb on a dish or board. Allow it to rest for 10 minutes. Remove the fat lumps.
5. Put butter on the buns, pile the lamb on the buns, and add pickle slices.
6. Serve it with black dip.

Special Mac And Cheese

👪 **Servings: 8**

🕐 **Cooking Time: 1 Hours**

Ingredients:

- 4 strips bacon, cooked crispy and chopped
- 2 cups breadcrumbs
- 2 tablespoons fresh parsley, minced
- Salt and pepper to taste
- 2 tablespoons olive oil
- 1 white onion, chopped
- 3 cloves garlic, crushed and minced
- 1/2 cup melted butter
- 5 tablespoons all-purpose flour
- 12 oz. cheddar cheese, shredded
- 4 oz. brie cheese
- 4 oz. mozzarella cheese, shredded
- 12 oz. raclette
- 8 oz. gruyere cheese, grated
- 1 cup heavy cream
- 4 oz. milk
- 8 cups cooked macaroni pasta
- 1 teaspoon freshly grated nutmeg

Directions:

1. In a bowl, mix the bacon bits, breadcrumbs, parsley, salt, and pepper. Set aside.
2. When ready to cook, turn the Traeger on and set the temperature to 350°F with the lid closed.
3. Pour the olive oil into a pan over medium heat.
4. Cook the onion and garlic for 2 minutes.
5. Add the jalapeño and cook for 1 more minute.
6. Stir in the butter and flour.
7. Cook while stirring for 5 minutes.
8. Add all the cheeses along with the cream and milk.
9. Reduce heat to low and cook while stirring for 7 minutes.
10. Add the pasta and stir to coat evenly with the sauce.
11. Season with the salt and pepper.
12. Pour the mixture to a cast-iron pan.
13. Cover with foil.
14. Place on top of the Traeger.
15. Bake for 20 minutes.
16. Sprinkle the breadcrumb mixture on top.
17. Bake for another 20 minutes.

Smoked Irish Bacon

👥 **Servings: 7**

🕐 **Cooking Time: 3 Hours**

Ingredients:

- 1 bay leaf
- 2/4 cup of water
- 2/3 cup of sugar
- 6 star anise, whole
- 1 cup of fresh fennel, preferably bulb and fronds
- 2 spring thyme, fresh
- 1 clove of garlic
- 2 tsp of curing salt
- 2-1/2 pound of pork loin
- 1-1/2 tsp of peppercorns, black
- 1-1/2 tsp of fennel seed

Directions:

1. In a big stockpot, mix the fennel seeds, peppercorn, star anise, and pork roast for about 3 minutes. Also, mix the sugar, water, thyme, garlic, curing salt, coarse salt, and bay leaves in a pot and, boil for 3 minutes until the salt and sugar dissolves.
2. Place the pork loin in a Ziploc bag, seal it, and put it in a roasting pan. Keep refrigerated for 4 days.
3. When ready to cook, turn the Traeger on and set the temperature to 250°F. Preheat the grill for 15 minutes at 250°F. Use pecan wood pellets.
4. Remove the pork from the brine and place on the grates of the grill. Smoke it for 2 hours 30 minutes or until internal temperature reads 145°F.
5. Serves immediately or when it is cool.

Fall Season Apple Pie

👥 **Servings: 8**

🕐 **Cooking Time: 1 Hours**

Ingredients:

- 8 C. apples, peeled, cored and sliced thinly
- ¾ C. sugar
- 1 tbsp. fresh lemon juice
- 1 tsp. ground cinnamon
- ¼ tsp. ground nutmeg
- 2 whole frozen pie crusts, thawed
- ¼ C. apple jelly
- 2 tbsp. apple juice
- 2 tbsp. heavy whipping cream

Directions:

1. When ready to cook, turn the Traeger on and set the temperature to 375°F and preheat with closed lid for 15 minutes.
2. In a bowl, add the apples, sugar, lemon juice, flour, cinnamon, and nutmeg and mix well.
3. Roll the pie crust dough into two (11-inch) circles.
4. Arrange 1 dough circle into a 9-inch pie plate.
5. Spread the apple jelly over dough evenly and top with apple mixture.
6. Dampen the edges of dough crust with apple juice.
7. Cover with the top crust, pressing the edges together to seal.
8. Trim the pastry, and flute the edges.
9. With a sparing knife, make several small slits in the top crust.
10. Brush the top of the pie with the cream.
11. Place the pie pan onto the grill and cook for about 50-60 minutes.
12. Remove from the grill and place the pie onto a wire rack to cool slightly.
13. Serve warm.

Summer Treat Corn

Servings: 6

Cooking Time: 20 Minutes

Ingredients:

- 6 fresh whole corn on the cob
- ½ C. butter
- Salt, to taste

Directions:

1. When ready to cook, turn the Traeger on and set the temperature to 400°F and preheat with closed lid for 15 minutes.
2. Husk the corn and remove all the silk.
3. Brush each corn with melted butter and sprinkle with salt.
4. Place the corn onto the grill and cook for about 20 minutes, rotating after every 5 minutes and brushing with butter once halfway through.
5. Serve warm.

Mouthwatering Cauliflower

Servings: 8

Cooking Time: 30 Minutes

Ingredients:

- 2 large heads cauliflower head, stem removed and cut into 2-inch florets
- 3 tbsp. olive oil
- Salt and freshly ground black pepper, to taste
- ¼ C. fresh parsley, chopped finely

Directions:

1. When ready to cook, turn the Traeger on and set the temperature to 500°F and preheat with closed lid for 15 minutes.
2. In a large bowl, add cauliflower florets, oil, salt and black pepper and toss to coat well.
3. Divide the cauliflower florets onto 2 baking sheets and spread in an even layer.
4. Place the baking sheets onto the grill and cook for about 20-30 minutes, stirring once after 15 minutes.
5. Remove the vegetables from grill and transfer into a large bowl.
6. Immediately, add the parsley and toss to coat well.
7. Serve immediately.

Cinnamon Sugar Donut Holes

👪 **Servings: 4**

🕐 **Cooking Time: 35 Minutes**

Ingredients:

- 1/2 cup flour
- 1tbsp cornstarch
- 1/2 tsp baking powder
- 1/8 tsp baking soda
- 1/8 tsp ground cinnamon
- 1/2 tsp kosher salt
- 1/4 cup buttermilk
- 1/4 cup sugar
- 11/2 tbsp butter, melted
- 1egg
- 1/2 tsp vanilla
- Topping
- 2tbsp sugar
- 1tbsp sugar
- 1tsp ground cinnamon

Directions:

1. When ready to cook, turn the Traeger on and set the temperature to 350°F.
2. In a medium bowl, combine flour, cornstarch, baking powder, baking soda, ground cinnamon, and kosher salt. Whisk to combine.
3. In a separate bowl, combine buttermilk, sugar, melted butter, egg, and vanilla. Whisk until the egg is thoroughly combined.
4. Pour wet mixture into the flour mixture and stir. Stir just until combined, careful not to overwork the mixture.
5. Spray mini muffin tin with cooking spray.
6. Spoon 1 tbsp of donut mixture into each mini muffin hole.
7. Place the tin on the pellet grill grate and bake for about 18 minutes, or until a toothpick can come out clean.
8. Remove muffin tin from the grill and let rest for about 5 minutes.
9. In a small bowl, combine 1 tbsp sugar and 1 tsp ground cinnamon.
10. Melt 2 tbsp of butter in a glass dish. Dip each donut hole in the melted butter, then mix and toss with cinnamon sugar. Place completed donut holes on a plate to serve.

Beer-braised Pork Shank

👪 **Servings:6**

🕐 **Cooking Time: 23 Minutes**

Ingredients:

- 2 Tbsp Flour
- Kosher salt
- Ground black pepper
- 2 Tbsp olive oil
- 2 Tbsp butter
- 1 medium onion, diced
- 2 carrots, trimmed and diced
- 1 Tbsp garlic, minced
- 1 cup dried mushrooms
- 2 cup beef broth
- 2 Tsp chili powder
- 2 thyme sprigs
- 2 Tsp coffee, instant
- 1 Tbsp Worcestershire sauce
- 12 oz dark beer, porter
- 2 dried bay leaves

Directions:

1. When ready to cook, turn the Traeger on and set the temperature to 300°F and preheat with the cover of the grill closed for 10 minutes.
2. Hold pork shank together with a butcher string and sprinkle pepper and salt over it.
3. Place a Dutch oven on the cooking grid. Add oil and pork shanks. Cook shank until brown on both sides.
4. Remove shanks from heat and transfer to a plate.
5. Sauté onions, carrots, and garlic in Dutch oven until tender, about 8 minutes.
6. Mix in beef broth, beer, and Worcestershire sauce to the sautéed vegetables. Increase the temperature and bring to boil. Allow simmering at Medium temperature until one-third of the liquid is gone.
7. Add tomato paste, coffee, thyme, chili powder, and bay leaves.
8. Transfer pork shanks from the plate into the Dutch oven and scoop sauce atop it.
9. Cook shanks until tender, about 3 hours.
10. Combine in a bowl, butter, and flour. Add the flour mixture in the last hours to thicken the sauce.
11. Take out bay leaves and thyme springs. Cut out butcher's string. Serve pork shank with gravy atop it and garnish with parsley.

Baked Breakfast Casserole

Servings: 8

Cooking Time: 1 Hours

Ingredients:

- 6 bread slices, cut into cubes
- 6 eggs
- 3/4 teaspoon ground mustard
- 1 cup milk
- Salt and pepper to taste
- 1 onion, chopped
- 1 bell pepper, chopped
- 6 ounces chorizo
- 6 ounces ground turkey
- 1 cup baby spinach
- 4 slices bacon, cooked crispy and chopped into bits
- 1 cup Swiss cheese, grated
- 2 cups cheddar cheese, grated

Directions:

1. When ready to cook, turn the Traeger on and set the temperature to 350°F.
2. Preheat for 15 minutes while the lid is closed.
3. Spray your baking pan with oil.
4. Arrange the bread cubes in the baking pan.
5. Beat the eggs in a bowl.
6. Stir in the mustard, milk, salt and pepper.
7. Spray your pan with oil.
8. Place the pan over medium heat.
9. Cook the onion, bell pepper, ground turkey and chorizo.
10. Stir in the spinach.
11. Cook for 1 minute.
12. Place the meat mixture on top of the bread.
13. Pour egg mixture on top.
14. Sprinkle cheeses on top.
15. Repeat layers.
16. Cover the baking pan with foil.
17. Bake in the Traeger for 40 minutes.
18. Remove cover and bake for another 10 minutes.

Grilled Tuna Burger With Ginger Mayonnaise

Servings: 4

Cooking Time: 20 Minutes

Ingredients:

- 1 Tbsp of sesame oil, optional
- 4 Tbsp of ginger, optional
- 4 hamburger buns
- Black pepper, freshly ground
- 2 Tbsp and 1 tsp of soy sauce
- 4 of 5 ounces of tuna steak
- Natural oil
- 1/2 cup of mayonnaise

Directions:

1. When ready to cook, turn the Traeger on and set the temperature to 300°F. Use maple pellets for a robust woody taste.
2. Rub soy sauce on the tuna steak and season with pepper.
3. In another bowl, prepare a rub by mixing the ginger, mayonnaise, 1 tsp of soy sauce, and sesame oil.
4. With a brush, apply the rub on the tuna steak then grill for 10 minutes before flipping. Grill the other side for another 10 minutes.
5. Serve immediately with fish between buns. Add mayonnaise and ginger as layers.

Barbecue Hot Dog

👪 **Servings: 6**

🕐 **Cooking Time: 10 Minutes**

Ingredients:

- 6 hot dogs
- ½ cup barbecue sauce
- 6 hot dog buns
- 1 onion, chopped
- ½ cup cheddar cheese, shredded

Directions:

1. When ready to cook, turn the Traeger on and set the temperature to 450°F. Preheat while the lid is closed for 10 minutes.
2. Grill the hot dogs for 5 minutes per side.
3. Brush the hot dogs with the barbecue sauce.
4. Serve in the hot dog buns topped with the onion and cheese.

Smoked Chuck Roast

👪 **Servings: 6**

🕐 **Cooking Time: 5 Hours**

Ingredients:

- 3 lb. chuck roast
- 3 tablespoons sweet and spicy rub
- 3 cups beef stock, divided
- 1 yellow onion, sliced

Directions:

1. Add the chuck roast to a baking pan.
2. Coat with the sweet, spicy rub.
3. Cover with foil. Refrigerate and marinate overnight.
4. When ready to cook, turn the Traeger on and set the temperature to 225°F.
5. Preheat it to 225°F.
6. Add the chuck roast to the grill.
7. Close the lid.
8. Smoke the chuck roast for 3 hours.
9. Brush with 1 cup beef stock every 1 hours.
10. Add the onion slices to a baking pan.
11. Pour the remaining beef stock.
12. Transfer the chuck roast on top of the onions.
13. Increase the heat to 250°F.
14. Smoke for 3 hours.
15. Cover the chuck roast with the foil.
16. Smoke for another 2 hours and 30 minutes.
17. Let the chuck roast rest for 10 minutes.

Traeger Smoked Sausage

👥 **Servings: 4 To 6**

🕐 **Cooking Time: 3 Hours**

Ingredients:

- 3 Pound ground pork
- 1/2 Tablespoon ground mustard
- 1 Tablespoon onion powder
- 1 Tablespoon garlic powder
- 1 Teaspoon pink curing salt
- 1 Tablespoon salt
- 4 Teaspoon black pepper
- 1/2 Cup ice water
- Hog casings, soaked and rinsed in cold water

Directions:

1. In a medium bowl, combine the meat and seasonings, mix well.
2. Add ice water to meat and mix with hands working quickly until everything is incorporated.
3. Place mixture in a sausage stuffer and follow manufacturer's instructions for operating. Use caution not to overstuff or the casing might burst.
4. Once all the meat is stuffed, determine your desired link length and pinch and twist a couple of times or tie it off. Repeat for each link.
5. When ready to cook, set Traeger temperature to 225 ℉ and preheat, lid closed for 15 minutes. For optimal flavor, use Super Smoke if available.
6. Place links directly on the grill grate and cook for 1 to 2 hours or until the internal temperature registers 155 ℉ . Let sausage rest a few minutes before slicing. Enjoy!

Twice-baked Spaghetti Squash

👥 **Servings: 2**

🕐 **Cooking Time:1 Hours 15 Minutes**

Ingredients:

- 1 medium spaghetti squash
- 1/2 cup of parmesan cheese (grated and divided)
- 1/2 cup of mozzarella cheese (shredded and divided)
- 1 tsp Salt
- Tbsp Extra-virgin olive oil
- 1/2 tsp Pepper

Directions:

1. When ready to cook, turn the Traeger on and set the temperature to 375°F. Using a knife, cut the squash into half lengthwise and remove the seed and pulp. Rub the inside of the squash with olive oil, salt, and pepper. Place on the hot grill with the open part facing up and bake for 45 minutes or until the squash can be easily pierced with a fork. Remove and allow to cool.
2. Place on a cutting board. Using a fork, scrape across the surface in a lengthwise direction to remove the flesh-in strand (to look like spaghetti). Transfer to a bowl, add parmesan and mozzarella cheese, then stir well. Stuff back into the shell, sprinkle cheese on the toppings.
3. Increase the pellet smoker-grill to 425°F, place the stuffed squash on the hot grill and bake for 15 minutes or until cheese starts to brown.
4. Remove and allow to cool, serve.

Bearnaise Sauce With Marinated London Broil

Servings: 4

Cooking Time: 50 Minutes

Ingredients:

- 2 cups of Rory's marinade
- 1-1/2 cups of béarnaise sauce
- 2-1/2 pound of London broil

Directions:

1. Place London broil in a big baking dish, pour marinade over the steak, then refrigerate it over the night.
2. When ready to cook, turn the Traeger on and set the temperature to 300°F. Use maple pellets for a robust woody taste.
3. Remove London broil from the marinade the following morning. Place it on the preheated grill and cook for 15 minutes before flipping and grilling the other side for 10 minutes. Serve immediately with béarnaise sauce.

Traeger Stuffed Burgers

Servings: 6

Cooking Time: 15 Minutes

Ingredients:

- 3 lb ground beef
- 1/2 tbsp onion powder
- 1/4 tbsp garlic powder
- 1 tbsp salt
- 1/2 tbsp pepper
- 1-1/2 cups Colby jack cheese, shredded
- Johnny's seasoning salt
- 6 slices Colby Jack cheese

Directions:

1. When ready to cook, turn the Traeger on and set the temperature to 375°F.
2. Mix beef, onion powder, garlic powder, salt, and pepper until well combined. Make 12 patties.
3. Place cheese on the burger patty and cover with another patty then seal the edges.
4. Season with salt, then place the patties on the grill. Cook the patties on the grill grate for 8 minutes, flip the patties and cook for additional 5 minutes.
5. Place a slice of cheese on each patty and grill with the lid closed to melt the cheese.
6. Remove the patties from the Traeger and let rest for 10 minutes. Serve and enjoy with a toasted bun.

Veggie Lover's Burgers

Servings: 6

Cooking Time: 51 Minutes

Ingredients:

- ¾ C. lentils
- 1 tbsp. ground flaxseed
- 2 tbsp. extra-virgin olive oil
- 1 onion, chopped
- 2 garlic cloves, minced
- Salt and freshly ground black pepper, to taste
- 1 C. walnuts, toasted
- ¾ C. breadcrumbs
- 1 tsp. ground cumin
- 1 tsp. paprika

Directions:

1. In a pan of boiling water, add the lentils and cook for about 15 minutes or until soft.
2. Drain the lentils completely and set aside.
3. In a small bowl, mix together the flaxseed with 4 tbsp. of water. Set aside for about 5 minutes.
4. In a medium skillet, heat the oil over medium heat and sauté the onion for about 4-6 minutes.
5. Add the garlic and a pinch of salt and pepper and sauté for about 30 seconds.
6. Remove from the heat and place the onion mixture into a food processor.
7. Add the ¾ of the lentils, flaxseed mixture, walnuts, breadcrumbs and spices and pulse until smooth.
8. Transfer the mixture into a bowl and gently, fold in the remaining lentils.
9. Make 6 patties from the mixture.
10. Place the patties onto a parchment paper-lined plate and refrigerate for at least 30 minutes.
11. When ready to cook, turn the Traeger on and set the temperature to 425°F and preheat with closed lid for 15 minutes, using charcoal.
12. Place the burgers onto the grill and cook for about 8-10 minutes flipping once halfway through.
13. Serve hot.

Bison Burgers

Servings: 6

Cooking Time: 17 To 19 Minutes

Ingredients:

- 2 pounds ground bison
- 2 tablespoons steak seasoning
- 4 tablespoons (½ stick) unsalted butter, cut into pieces
- 1 large onion, finely minced
- 6 slices Swiss cheese
- 6 ciabatta buns, split
- Sweet and Spicy Jalapeño Relish, for serving
- Lettuce and sliced tomatoes, for serving

Directions:

1. When ready to cook, turn the Traeger on and set the temperature to 425°F. Preheat, with the lid closed, to 425°F.
2. In a large bowl, combine the ground bison and steak seasoning until well blended.
3. Shape the meat mixture into 6 patties and make a thumb indentation in the center of each. Set aside.
4. Place a rimmed baking sheet on the grill and add the butter and onion. Sauté for 5 minutes, or until the onion is translucent. Top with the bison burger patties, indention-side down.
5. Close the lid and smoke for 6 to 7 minutes, then flip the burgers and smother them in the sautéed onion. Close the lid again and continue smoking for 6 to 7 minutes. During the last few minutes of cooking, top each burger with a slice of Swiss cheese. For safe consumption, the internal temperature should reach between 140°F (medium) and 160°F (well-done).
6. Lightly toast the ciabatta buns, split-side down, on one side of the smoker.
7. Serve the onion-smothered cheeseburgers on the toasted buns with jalapeño relish, lettuce, and tomato—or whatever toppings you like.

Roasted Steak

👪 **Servings: 5**

🕐 **Cooking Time: 12 Hours 30 Minutes**

Ingredients:

- 2 Tbsp of rosemary, preferably freshly chopped
- 2 tsp of salt
- 1 Tbsp of thyme, preferably fresh leaves
- 1/2 cup of olive oil
- 1-1/2 tsp of black pepper
- 1 of 3-inch steak
- 5 cloves of garlic, preferably thinly sliced

Directions:

1. Make the marinade by cooking garlic until it is soft, then add rosemary and thyme. Cook for about 1 minute.
2. Rub black pepper and salt all over the steak, then put it inside a Ziploc bag with the garlic mixture. Keep in the refrigerator overnight.
3. Remove steak from the refrigerator the next morning, and discard the garlic marinade. When ready to cook, turn the Traeger on and set the temperature to 160°F. Roast the steak on the preheated grill for 30 minutes or until the internal temperature reads 160°F.
4. Serve the steak and season with salt and black pepper before eating.

Grilled Lime Chicken

👪 **Servings: 6**

🕐 **Cooking Time: 45 Minutes**

Ingredients:

- 2 teaspoon sugar
- 1 teaspoon chili powder
- 1 1/2 teaspoons granulated garlic
- 1 1/2 teaspoons ground cumin
- Salt and pepper to taste
- 12 chicken thighs, skin removed
- 1 1/2 tablespoons olive oil
- 1 1/2 tablespoons butter
- 4 tablespoons pineapple juice
- 4 tablespoons honey
- 1 1/2 tablespoons lime juice
- 1/4 teaspoon red pepper flakes
- 1 1/2 tablespoons hot sauce

Directions:

1. When ready to cook, turn the Traeger on and set the temperature to 375°F.
2. Preheat it for 10 minutes.
3. In a bowl, mix the sugar, chili powder, garlic, cumin, salt and pepper.
4. Coat the chicken with the olive oil and sprinkle with the dry rub.
5. Grill the chicken for 7 minutes per side.
6. In a pan over medium heat, simmer the rest of the ingredients for 10 minutes.
7. Remove from heat and transfer to a bowl.
8. Brush the mixture on both sides of the chicken.
9. Cook for another 7 minutes per side.

Baked Apple Crisp

👥 **Servings: 7**

🕐 **Cooking Time: 30 Minutes**

Ingredients:

- Butter for greasing
- 1/2 cup flour
- 1/2 cup rolled oats
- 1 stick butter, sliced into cubes
- 1 cup brown sugar
- 1 1/2 teaspoon ground cinnamon
- 1/4 cup walnuts, chopped
- 3 lb. apples, sliced thinly
- ½ cup dried cranberries
- 2 1/2 tablespoons bourbon
- 1/2 cup brown sugar
- 1 tablespoon lemon juice
- 1/4 cup honey
- 1 teaspoon vanilla
- 1 1/2 teaspoons ground cinnamon
- Pinch salt

Directions:

1. Grease cast iron pan with butter.
2. Add flour, oats, butter cubes, 1 cup sugar, cinnamon and walnuts to a food processor. Pulse until crumbly.
3. In a bowl, mix the apples with the rest of the ingredients.
4. Pour apple mixture into the greased pan.
5. Spread flour mixture on top.
6. When ready to cook, turn the Traeger on and set the temperature to 350°F. Bake in the Traeger at 350°F for 1 hours.

Seafood On Skewers

👥 **Servings: 4**

🕐 **Cooking Time: 40 Minutes**

Ingredients:

- 2 Tbsp of peanuts or corn oil
- 16 cubes of swordfish
- 8 sea scallops, big
- Salt and ground pepper, fresh
- 16 cubes of monkfish
- 12 jumbo shrimp
- Sauce Bearnaise

Directions:

1. When ready to cook, turn the Traeger on and set the temperature to 200°F. Use oak wood pellets for rich, woody taste.
2. Arrange four pieces of alternating swordfish and monkfish pieces, shrimps, and scallops on a metal skewer. Repeat this for the other three skewers. Rub oil on the skewers.
3. Place the skewers on the preheated grill, and cook for 10 minutes. Flip to the other side and season with salt and pepper. Allow the other side to cook for another 10 minutes. Serve it with béarnaise sauce.

Smoked Pork Cutlets With Caraway And Dill

Servings: 4

Cooking Time: 1 Hours And 45 Minutes

Ingredients:

- 4 pork cutlets
- 2 lemons freshly squeezed
- 2 Tbs fresh parsley finely chopped
- 1 Tbsp of ground caraway
- 3 Tbsp of fresh dill finely chopped
- 1/4 cup of olive oil
- Salt and ground black pepper

Directions:

1. Place the pork cutlets in a bag along and shake to combine well. Refrigerate for at least 4 hours.
2. Remove the pork cutlets from marinade and pat dry
3. When ready to cook, turn the Traeger on and set the temperature to 250°F.
4. Arrange pork cutlets on the grill rack and smoke for about 1 1/2 hours. Allow cooling on room temperature before serving.

Cornish Game Hens

Servings: 6

Cooking Time: 1 Hours

Ingredients:

- 4 Cornish game hens, giblets removed
- 4 teaspoons chicken rub
- 4 sprigs of rosemary
- 4 tablespoons butter, unsalted, melted

Directions:

1. Switch on the Traeger grill, fill the grill hopper with mesquite flavored wood pellets, power the grill on by using the control panel, select 'smoke' on the temperature dial, or when ready to cook, turn the Traeger on and set the temperature to 375°F and let it preheat for a minimum of 15 minutes.
2. Meanwhile, rinse the hens, pat dry with paper towels, tie the wings by using a butcher's strong, then rub evenly with melted butter, sprinkle with chicken rub and stuff cavity of each hen with a rosemary sprig.
3. When the grill has preheated, open the lid, place hens on the grill grate, shut the grill, and smoke for 1 hours until thoroughly cooked and internal temperature reaches 165°F.
4. When done, transfer hens to a dish, let rest for 5 minutes and then serve.

Smoked Pork Shoulder

👥 **Servings: 8**

🕐 **Cooking Time: 7 Hours**

Ingredients:

- 2 tsp of garlic powder
- 4 tsp of salt, either sea and kosher
- 2 tsp of onion powder
- 4 tsp of black pepper
- 2 tsp of garlic
- 6 pounds of pork shoulder
- 1 tsp of cayenne pepper
- Carolina vinegar sauce
- 11 sesame seed buns, already split
- 3 Tbsp of melted butter.

Directions:

1. When ready to cook, turn the Traeger on and set the temperature to 245°F. Preheat the grill for 15 minutes at 245°F. Use apple wood pellets for a distinctive, strong woody taste.
2. Mix onion powder, pepper, garlic powder, cayenne, salt, and black pepper in a bowl. Use your fingers to rub the mixture on the meat.
3. Place the pork shoulder inside the grill and smoke for 7 hours.
4. Slice the pork, and the bones will remove effortlessly.
5. Put the shredded pork in a plate, add sauce and stir it together
6. Serve it with butter and toasted buns.

Grilled Chicken With Lemon & Cumin

👥 **Servings: 4**

🕐 **Cooking Time: 10 Minutes**

Ingredients:

- 4 chicken breast fillets
- 2 teaspoons olive oil
- 4 teaspoons ground cumin
- 2 tablespoons lemon juice
- 1 tablespoon lime juice
- Salt and pepper to taste

Directions:

1. Coat the chicken breast with oil.
2. In a bowl, mix the rest of the ingredients.
3. Brush the chicken breast with the lemon and cumin mixture.
4. Cover and marinate in the refrigerator for 3 hours.
5. When ready to cook, turn the Traeger on and set the temperature to 350°F.
6. Preheat for 15 minutes while the lid is closed.
7. Grill the chicken for 5 minutes per side.
8. Let rest for 5 minutes before serving.

Spiced Nuts

Servings: 32

Cooking Time: 20 Minutes

Ingredients:

- 1teaspoon dried rosemary
- 1/8 teaspoon cayenne pepper
- 1/8 teaspoon ground black pepper
- ½ teaspoon salt or to taste
- ½ teaspoon ground cuminutes
- 1tablespoon olive oil
- 2tablespoon maple syrup
- 2/3 cup raw and unsalted cashew nuts
- 2/3 cup raw and unsalted pecans
- 2/3 cup raw and unsalted walnuts

Directions:

1. Start your grill on smoke mode, leaving the lid open for 5 minutes, until the fire starts.
2. Close the grill lid. When ready to cook, turn the Traeger on and set the temperature to 350°F.
3. In a large bowl, combine all the ingredients except the dried rosemary. Mix thoroughly until the ingredients are evenly mixed, and all nuts are coated with spices.
4. Spread the spiced nuts on a baking sheet.
5. Place the baking sheet on the grill and roast the nuts for 20 to 25 minutes.
6. Remove the nuts from heat.
7. Sprinkle the dried rosemary on the nuts and stir to mix.
8. Leave the nuts to cool for a few minutes.
9. Serve and enjoy.

Succulent Lamb Chops

Servings: 4 To 6

Cooking Time: 10 To 20 Minutes

Ingredients:

- ½ cup rice wine vinegar
- 1 teaspoon liquid smoke
- 2 tablespoons extra-virgin olive oil
- 2 tablespoons dried minced onion
- 1 tablespoon chopped fresh mint
- 8 (4-ounce) lamb chops
- ½ cup hot pepper jelly
- 1 tablespoon Sriracha
- 1 teaspoon salt
- 1 teaspoon freshly ground black pepper

Directions:

1. In a small bowl, whisk together the rice wine vinegar, liquid smoke, olive oil, minced onion, and mint. Place the lamb chops in an aluminum roasting pan. Pour the marinade over the meat, turning to coat thoroughly. Cover with plastic wrap and marinate in the refrigerator for 2 hours.
2. When ready to cook, turn the Traeger on and set the temperature to 165°F. Preheat, with the lid closed, to 165°F, or the "Smoke" setting.
3. On the stove top, in a small saucepan over low heat, combine the hot pepper jelly and Sriracha and keep warm.
4. When ready to cook the chops, remove them from the marinade and pat dry. Discard the marinade.
5. Season the chops with the salt and pepper, then place them directly on the grill grate, close the lid, and smoke for 5 minutes to "breathe" some smoke into them.
6. Remove the chops from the grill. Increase the pellet cooker temperature to 450°F, or the "High" setting. Once the grill is up to temperature, place the chops on the grill and sear, cooking for 2 minutes per side to achieve medium-rare chops. A meat thermometer inserted in the thickest part of the meat should read 145°F. Continue grilling, if necessary, to your desired doneness.
7. Serve the chops with the warm Sriracha pepper jelly on the side.

Smoked Bananas Foster Bread Pudding

Servings: 8 To 10

Cooking Time: 2 Hours 15 Minutes

Ingredients:

- 1loaf (about 4 cups) brioche or challah, cubed to 1 inch cubes
- 3eggs, lightly beaten
- 2cups of milk
- 2/3 cups sugar
- 2large bananas, peeled and smashed
- 1tbsp vanilla extract
- 1tbsp cinnamon
- 1/4 tsp nutmeg
- 1/2 cup pecans
- Rum Sauce Ingredients:
- 1/2 cup spiced rum
- 1/4 cup unsalted butter
- 1cup dark brown sugar
- 1tsp cinnamon
- 5large bananas, peeled and quartered

Directions:

1. Place pecans on a skillet over medium heat and lightly toast for about 5 minutes, until you can smell them.
2. Remove from heat and allow to cool. Once cooled, chop pecans.
3. Lightly butter a 9" x 13" baking dish and evenly layer bread cubes in the dish.
4. In a large bowl, whisk eggs, milk, sugar, mashed bananas, vanilla extract, cinnamon, and nutmeg until combined.
5. Pour egg mixture over the bread in the baking dish evenly. Sprinkle with chopped pecans. Cover with aluminum foil and refrigerate for about 30 minutes.
6. When ready to cook, turn the Traeger on and set the temperature to 180°F.
7. Remove foil from dish and place on the smoker for 5 minutes with the lid closed, allowing bread to absorb smoky flavor.
8. Remove dish from the grill and cover with foil again. Increase your pellet grill's temperature to 350°F.
9. Place dish on the grill grate and cook for 50-60 minutes until everything is cooked through and the bread pudding is bubbling.
10. In a saucepan, while pudding cooks heat up butter for rum sauce over medium heat. When the butter begins to melt, add the brown sugar, cinnamon, and bananas. Sauté until bananas begin to soften.
11. Add rum and watch. When the liquid begins to bubble, light a match, and tilt the pan. Slowly and carefully move the match towards the liquid until the sauce lights. When the flames go away, remove skillet from heat.
12. If you're uncomfortable lighting the liquid with a match, just cook it for 3-4 minutes over medium heat after the rum has been added.
13. Keep rum sauce on a simmer or reheat once it's time to serve.
14. Remove bread pudding from the grill and allow it to cool for about 5 minutes.
15. Cut into squares, put each square on a plate and add a piece of banana then drizzle rum sauce over the top. Serve on its own or a la mode and enjoy it!

RECIPE INDEX INDEX

A

Applewood-smoked Whole Turkey 33

Aromatic Herbed Rack Of Lamb 9

Authentic Holiday Turkey Breast 35

B

Bacon-wrapped Chicken Tenders 45

Bacon-wrapped Sausages In Brown Sugar 19

Baked Apple Crisp 107

Baked Breakfast Casserole 101

Barbecue Chicken Wings 51

Barbecue Hot Dog 102

Barbecued Tenderloin 23

Barbeque Shrimp 75

Bbq Breakfast Grits 8

Bbq Half Chickens 39

Bbq Sweet Pepper Meatloaf 17

Bearnaise Sauce With Marinated London Broil 104

Beer-braised Pork Shank 100

Bison Burgers 105

Blackened Catfish 56

Blackened Steak 14

Blt Pasta Salad 88

Budget Friendly Chicken Legs 38

Buffalo Chicken Flatbread 39

Buffalo Chicken Wraps 42

Buttered Crab Legs 76

Buttermilk Pork Loin Roast 12

C

Cajun Chicken 48

Cajun-blackened Shrimp 72

Chilean Sea Bass 70

Chinese Inspired Duck Legs 50

Cider Salmon 62

Cinco De Mayo Chicken Enchiladas 41

Cinnamon Sugar Donut Holes 100

Citrus Salmon 74

Citrus-smoked Trout 58

Classic Pulled Pork 25

Cod With Lemon Herb Butter 64

Competition Style Bbq Pork Ribs 6

Cornish Game Hens 108

Cowboy Cut Steak 13

Crazy Delicious Lobster Tails 72

Crispy & Juicy Chicken 36

Crispy Maple Bacon Brussels Sprouts 79

D

Deliciously Spicy Rack Of Lamb 7

Drunken Beef Jerky 18

E

Easy Smoked Vegetables 85

Easy-to-prepare Lamb Chops 8

F

Fall Season Apple Pie 98

Feisty Roasted Cauliflower 91

Flavor-bursting Prawn Skewers 57

G

Game Day Chicken Drumsticks 32

Garlic And Herb Smoke Potato 87

Garlic Parmesan Chicken Wings 34

Georgia Sweet Onion Bake 83

Grilled Baby Carrots And Fennel With Romesco 78

Grilled Blackened Salmon 76

Grilled Carrots And Asparagus 82

Grilled Cherry Tomato Skewers 79

Grilled Chicken With Lemon & Cumin 109

Grilled Chili Burger 95

Grilled Corn With Honey & Butter 83

Grilled Lime Chicken 106

Grilled Lingcod 62

Grilled Pepper Steak With Mushroom Sauce 96

Grilled Potato Salad 86

Grilled Rainbow Trout 74

Grilled Ratatouille Salad 80

Grilled Salmon 71

Grilled Shrimp Scampi 65

Grilled Tilapia 60

Grilled Tuna 60

Grilled Tuna Burger With Ginger Mayonnaise 101

Grilled Venison Kebab 95

H

Halibut 68

Herb Roasted Turkey 47

Hot-smoked Salmon 69

J

Jamaican Jerk Chicken Quarters 43

Jerk Shrimp 63

L

Lamb Breast 10

Lamb Shank 6

Leg Of A Lamb 25

Lemon Garlic Scallops 57

Lively Flavored Shrimp 56

Lobster Tails 70

M

Mango Shrimp 71

Maple And Bacon Chicken 54

Midweek Dinner Pork Tenderloin 27

Mouthwatering Cauliflower 99

Mutton Barbecued And Black Dip 97

O

Omega-3 Rich Salmon 65

Oysters In The Shell 59

P

Pacific Northwest Salmon 73

Paprika Chicken 36

Pork Belly Burnt Ends 24

Potato Fries With Chipotle Peppers 90

R

Recipes 77

Reverse-seared Steaks 18

Roast Beef 20

Roasted Okra 93

Roasted Parmesan Cheese Broccoli 87

Roasted Pork With Balsamic Strawberry Sauce 16

Roasted Pork With Blackberry Sauce 15

Roasted Root Vegetables 93

Roasted Spicy Tomatoes 88

Roasted Steak 106

Roasted Vegetable Medley 81

Roasted Veggies & Hummus 92

Roasted Whole Ham In Apricot Sauce 12

S

Santa Maria Tri-tip 7

Savory-sweet Turkey Legs 33

Seafood On Skewers 107

Serrano Chicken Wings 37

Simple Grilled Lamb Chops 20

Simply Delicious Tri Tip Roast 22

Skinny Smoked Chicken Breasts 48

Smo-fried Chicken 32

Smoked And Fried Chicken Wings 44

Smoked Apple Bbq Ribs 23

Smoked Bananas Foster Bread Pudding 111

Smoked Beef Ribs 24

Smoked Chicken Drumsticks 37

Smoked Chuck Roast 102

Smoked Cornish Chicken In Wood Pellets 34

Smoked Deviled Eggs 81

Smoked Fried Chicken 53

Smoked Healthy Cabbage 80

Smoked Irish Bacon 98

Smoked Longhorn Cowboy Tri-tip 21

Smoked Midnight Brisket 17

Smoked New York Steaks 15

Smoked Porchetta With Italian Salsa Verde 29

Smoked Pork Cutlets With Caraway And Dill 108

Smoked Pork Shoulder 109

Smoked Pork Tenderloin   14

Smoked Rack Of Lamb   9

Smoked Scallops   58

Smoked Teriyaki Tuna   96

Smoked Tofu   86

Smoked Trip Tip With Java Chophouse   16

Smoked Turkey Breast   49

Smoked Turkey Wings   46

Smoked Whole Chicken   47

Smoking Duck With Mandarin Glaze   52

South-east-asian Chicken Drumsticks   43

Southern Sugar-glazed Ham   10

Spatchcocked Turkey   41

Special Mac And Cheese   97

Spiced Nuts   110

Sriracha Salmon   61

St. Patrick Day's Corned Beef   28

Strip Steak With Onion Sauce   19

Stunning Prime Rib Roast   11

Succulent Lamb Chops   110

Summer Treat Corn   99

Super-tasty Trout   61

Supper Beef Roast   26

Sweet And Spicy Smoked Wings   52

Sweet Jalapeño Cornbread   91

Sweet Potato Fries   90

Sweet Sriracha Bbq Chicken   40

T

Teriyaki Smoked Shrimp   63

Texas Shoulder Clod   27

Texas-style Beef Ribs   26

Thanksgiving Dinner Turkey   50

Togarashi Smoked Salmon   66

Traeger Beef Short Rib Lollipop   11

Traeger Smoked Sausage   103

Traeger Stuffed Burgers   104

Twice-baked Spaghetti Squash   103

U

Ultimate Tasty Chicken   49

V

Veggie Lover's Burgers   105

W

Whole Roasted Cauliflower With Garlic Parmesan Butter   78

Wine Braised Lamb Shank   28

Wine Infused Salmon   59

Wood Pellet Bacon Wrapped Jalapeno Poppers   84

Wood Pellet Chicken Breasts   44

Wood Pellet Chile Lime Chicken   42

Wood Pellet Garlic Dill Smoked Salmon   67

Wood Pellet Grill Deli-style Roast Beef   30

Wood Pellet Grill Pork Crown Roast   22

Wood Pellet Grill Spicy Sweet Potatoes   89

Wood Pellet Grilled Asparagus And Honey Glazed Carrots   89

Wood Pellet Grilled Bacon   21

Wood Pellet Grilled Buffalo Chicken   46

Wood Pellet Grilled Buffalo Chicken Leg   45

Wood Pellet Grilled Chicken   38

Wood Pellet Grilled Lobster Tail   66

Wood Pellet Grilled Mexican Street Corn   85

Wood Pellet Grilled Salmon Sandwich   64

Wood Pellet Grilled Vegetables   92

Wood Pellet Grilled Zucchini Squash Spears   84

Wood Pellet Rockfish   75

Wood Pellet Salt And Pepper Spot Prawn Skewers   68

Wood Pellet Smoked Acorn Squash   82

Wood Pellet Smoked Brisket   13

Wood Pellet Smoked Buffalo Shrimp   67

Wood Pellet Smoked Cornish Hens   53

Wood Pellet Smoked Spatchcock Turkey   35

Wood Pellet Smoked Spatchcock Turkey   40

Wood Pellet Teriyaki Smoked Shrimp   73

Wood-fired Chicken Breasts   51

Wood-fired Halibut   69

CPSIA information can be obtained
at www.ICGtesting.com
Printed in the USA
LVHW011949080622
720773LV00003B/32

9 781803 676258